# ENOUGHNESS

## Finding True Fulfillment
## & Living a Fully Expressed Life

JASON A. WEISGERBER

# ENOUGHNESS

## Finding Fulfillment & Living a Fully Expressed Life

*Part Memoir, Part Meditation, Part Return to Innocence*

# Jason A. Weisgerber

Enoughness
© January 2016
By Jason A. Weisgerber

For more information contact :
www.EnoughnessSessions.com
Jason@JasonWeisgerber.com

Cover art by: Pixel Studio
Interior layout by: Melissa@TheWriterLab.com

Printed in the United States of America
First Printing, January 2016

ISBN-13: 978-1518726019
ISBN-10: 1518726011

# DEDICATION

I dedicate this book my family, friends and colleagues that have been a massive support along the way. You know who you are. Know that I thank you now and I've silently thanked you each and every moment for your encouragement, understanding and love. I couldn't have done this without you. This marks the completion of a long journey in my life. I'm so glad to consider you an important part of the guidance and support I needed to come to completion and beyond. My thanks and love to you.

I also dedicate this book to you the reader. May you live truly fulfilled and fully expressed in your own experience of Enoughness!

# CONTENTS

# PRELUDE

## The Promise of Enoughness

There's something that's good to hear at any age, from any background and in any situation. It's the promise of Enoughness.

Perhaps for too long you've been the 'child' waiting, longing - alone and in the dark - as if a 'parent' of yours has long been missing. When they finally do return, as was the promise, they look at you and say...

*You are enough.*
*Right here and right now,*
*you, as you are,*
*as you have been since hour one,*
*are enough.*

*You are enough for a full and flourishing life.*
*Live now the way you have always wanted to live*

*if only you believed in yourself.*
*Now is the time to believe.*

⟋⟋

*Take no more luxury in doubt,*
*waste no more time in confusion.*
*Hold nothing back.*
*Come fully forward now into your life.*

⟋⟋

*Enoughness is your return to innocence.*
*It is the return to your true and natural strength,*
*no matter your history or circumstance.*
*It is your birthright to a full and flourishing life.*

⟋⟋

*Enoughness is the pre-existing elixir running through your veins.*
*It is the heat and the blood that beats true in your heart.*
*Feel it now. Live it now.*

⟋⟋

*Let Enoughness resound within you.*
*Let it fill every crack and crevice.*

# Enoughness

*Let it be like the rippling rings of a stone dropped in still water*
*reaching across to touch every inch of the surrounding shore.*

⁓

*Now stand fast.*
*Enoughness is not merely a soft state of survival.*
*It is not a lazy complacency or a partial recovery from defeat.*
*Enoughness is not a presumptuous, pretentious, easy assumption*
*to be frivolously spoken but never truly lived.*

⁓

*Enoughness is yours,*
*yet you must reach with courage into your heart,*
*stand your feet strong on the earth*
*and rightly claim it for yourself.*

⁓

*This is not an end.*
*Enoughness is always and forever more*
*a beginning. Your beginning.*

⁓

*Like the acorn that becomes the oak,*
*the under dog that becomes the dark horse,*

*the caterpillar, the butterfly ~*
*let Enoughness be the nudge that cracks open your chysilas*
*to fully spread your wings*
*and fly.*

~~

*Feel this pure and natural strength within you now*
*like the fiber and muscle of the earths' cosmic tissue*
*and the suns undying brilliance.*
*Wield it with grace ~ not force.*

~~

*Remember this call.*
*Remember what it FEELS like to be truly ALIVE.*
*And always always always - remember your Enoughness.*

# INTRODUCTION

In my early thirties, I had a breakdown at 2am in a Los Angeles city park. Breakdown - breakthrough. Right in the middle of the night, right in the middle of the park, right in the middle of my life, I fell apart. It was the right thing to do.

I'd wandered down a dead end and had lived a deadened life - long enough. Ten years in Hollywood in pursuit of a dream. Not a unique dream, but a dream nonetheless, to become a professional actor. And frankly, to escape myself. I was nothing. I wanted to make something of myself, of my life and touch glory. Didn't happen. All was lost. Dead ends suck. Credit for staying committed.

Nobody knew it was happening, not even me - the breaking down. It happens over years not days. I knew something was off. Something inside me wasn't right. My spirit was broken. My heart was empty. My vision was lost. Something.

And in the end, there were only two choices: stop or...maybe there weren't two choices. Yet.

Falling apart was the greatest thing that ever happened to me. It was the first feel of a new life – a new life lived beyond the crippling insecurity, depression and doubt that had followed me for years. It was the first feel of a new life lived in and from the newfound perspective of *Enoughness*.

First, I had to let it all go. In the park. At 2am.

I gave up, dropped to the ground and wept. Furiously.

Then - time stopped. And then - *relief*. Profound relief. Not perfection, not glory...just...relief.

I've always wanted that to happen. Stop time. Get clean. I could choose a different direction, a different life, if I could just really stop for a minute, dust myself off and look around. Which is what I did. Accidentally.

In that sudden stillness was what felt like a full pause. It was a desperately needed release from the shame of failure and the feelings of haunting emptiness. It was all slowly killing me and driving me to the brink of suicide. And I was tired of being driven, pushed. I was ready to end it. Luckily, I was given a peek beyond the brink.

Funny. I remember feeling this kind of ballooning pain when I had a severe ear infection at 6 years old. Just like in the park, the pain was taking me over. I couldn't escape it.

My mother, a nurse by trade, tried helplessly to relieve my pain. But in the end, we had to let nature take its course. My eardrum burst. The pain was excruciating and almost knocked me out. It was also the sudden bliss-filled relief I needed.

The pain was gone. I didn't care how it happened. I was just happy it was over! With a giant dopey smile, I jumped off the bed and back into my innocence, baptized by pain and born into glory.

The same was true (yet in a slightly more profound way) for the existential relief I experienced in that Los Angeles park some 25 years later. This time, for a few precious moments, it was the cloud-heavy weight of depression and anxiety-ridden desperation that disappeared. It had built up after years of rejection, failure and creeping desperation.

It was true. I was a failed actor. In Hollywood. *I was at the very heart of desperation.* After a 10-year effort, I was broke emotionally, physically, financially and spiritually. I had to quit. And I was ashamed.

It wasn't just that. My whole life had been a painful effort to find meaning, to have value, to have a path, to find a voice and to be heard. And it relentlessly remained elusive.

I've always felt silent, invisible and unknown not only to the world but also to myself. After all these years, all this effort, I still didn't know. I didn't know where I belonged or who I was. It was always on the tip of my tongue, and though I tried, I couldn't quite get it out. It was time to give up. My fatigue had peaked.

Yet there in the aftermath of sweet release, my feelings of worthlessness, voiceless-ness, self-loathing and a chronic insecurity that stretched back to my childhood, stopped. I suddenly and unreasonably felt like I belonged in the world, like I had a place and purpose for the first time. And I had no idea about the specifics. It didn't matter. It was simply the *feel* of belonging, purpose, value and meaning that came in. And that made all the difference.

In that moment I didn't feel like the victim, the lost child or the confused one. I felt...older than that. And newer. Bigger.

In place of inner conflict came a momentary peace and a dumbfounded joy I'd never felt before. It felt good being dumb and founded. It felt like a renewal, a baptism, a return to innocence. It felt *completion.*

Though it was brief, I was at peace.

# Enoughness

Then there came a reckoning - a reckoning from within. It was the pure feeling of inherent value and strength, independent of my history, circumstance, success or failure. It was the feeling of personal value beyond any reason. It was a timeless reminder and a vital last minute wake up call.

For years, and only moments before, I'd been a camel in Alaska. I'd always felt uncomfortable, vulnerable and out of my element. In school, at home and on the planet. For years, I'd looked hard but I couldn't find any way in or any way out. And now I couldn't see any other way than taking my own life. *It almost seemed logical.*

This momentary relief was an opportunity to make one simple decision – to live or die. It was an opportunity to finally have a say in the shape of things. The decision was totally and completely up to me. And that gave me strength.

I chose life. I *chose...*life.

The *Enoughness* epiphany was clearly a turning point in my life. There was new light where before there was darkness. Even though the 'light' was only on for an instant, it was enough. Even though I'd have to turn it on again and again and again, it was enough just to find the switch.

If I were a camel in Alaska, now I had an igloo. And a lamp.

The impression was made. And thankfully, with some work, it would last. I felt humbled, blessed and good. I was awake in my own skin, in my own life. I would eventually find a way to stretch fully into that power and recall it at-will.

Soon, rather than a career, a person or a bank account; appearances, fame or fortune; I'd make a *feeling* (the one I call Enoughness) the biggest priority in my life. And I'd do it by facing my fears, short-comings, doubts and insecurities - embracing them rather than overcoming, pushing down, covering up or hiding them. And I'd find my strength again.

Through the experience of Enoughness, I've learned that insecurity, just like the wind, doesn't go away. I'm human; I'm always going to feel afraid and alone to some degree. I no longer feel the need to escape it. It comes and it goes. There are tornadoes and there are gentle spring breezes. I find flow in the ever-changing winds of life. Enoughness - has become my sail.

# 1

# THROUGH THE EYES OF ILLUMINATION

It's 2 AM in Los Angeles and I've just come out of a double-header movie in a futile attempt to escape the relentless frustration I've been living under for years. Not living, surviving. I know you know what I mean.

At 34 years old, I'm still unwittingly trying to shake off the lingering pain of a violent knifepoint attack at 11 years old, the failure of my acting pursuits and a numbing depression that has defined me for years. And now, even after the distraction of back-to-back late night movies, I'm feeling worse than ever. Movies are and have always been my favorite way to get lost, dream and find hope. Usually distracting myself like this works to buy me a few days, or hours, of solace. Not this time.

As I'm walking home through the nearby park, I have to stop. I can't take another step. I'm done. I'm done struggling, chasing, fighting, losing, failing…falling.

At this point, taking my own life doesn't seem tragic to me. It's more than an escape. In a strangely encouraging way, it seems like a real taste of triumph.

But I know it's not. I know it won't be. I keep running into what my Dad always says – *in life, there are no short cuts. And don't stand there like you're being milked!* Do something. So I did.

Out of pure frustration, I fall to my knees in a sobbing rage. The thought of someone seeing me lose it in the middle of this park, in the middle of the night, doesn't matter. Everything is blocked out. I'm screaming, yelling, spitting, crying and punching at the ground, at myself, at God, at everything. I want it to stop!

I let it all out…and collapse.

Suddenly everything gets very quiet - very still. As I kneel there on the ground exhausted, I'm starting to feel…relief. I'm starting to feel *only* relief.

All the pain, emptiness and confusion - the depression and the desperation – all stop and drop away.

I look up. The park is illuminated.

This isn't an external light but a 'light' that seems to be coming from within. A glow. Rather than just seeing it with my eyes, I feel it with my entire being. I feel it strong like a child. The grass, rocks, trees, and even the birds are illuminated, alive, *animated* all around me. Time slows way down.

It all feels personal, close and...personal. Intimate. And I'm kind of...talking with it all, being with it and feeling very much a part of it all. New to me.

I'm *resting* in it now. Breathing. Just breathing. I feel...peace. I feel complete. I feel whole. I feel at home.

I'm not crazy. I hope. And I'm not shocked. I'm too weary for shock. But I'm open. Mother Nature wants to have a direct conversation with me right here and right now. But I'm too tired to stand. It'll have to be right here on my knees. I'm listening.

My whole body begins to grow warm in this communion. Light...life...seems to be pouring into me. And for the first time in a long time, I realize I'm not alone. I'm feeling...different. I'm feeling connected. I'm feeling...right.

I'm enjoying the slowness. And I feel an excitement begin to build in the center of my chest. *Epiphany.* It seems I have access to the universal mind, to the meaning for which I've been unwittingly and desperately searching. Questions come.

*Why. Why am I like this? Why are we like this? Why this pain without cause? Pain seems to be the only thing that lasts in life. Why? Why is it not easier to feel joy, peace, ease, strength, happiness, love?*

I can't help but break the 'silence' and ask these burning (and human) questions that have plagued me these many years.

*What is all this suffering and pain? Is there a purpose to it? Is there a reason for hurting so much? Is there meaning to my own, my family's, to everyone's seemingly unavoidable pain? Why so much suffering? Why so many unlived lives? Why so many broken? Why so many lonely and unfulfilled? Is there another way!? Is there a reason to it all? And if so, who's pulling the strings!? I want to have a talk with them!*

And from somewhere deep within and all around me, my questions are answered. Soothed. Unburdened. *Yes...Be still.*

It's more of a *feeling* than a literal answer. *Yes...Be still.* Though I don't quite get it, I feel received. I'm at ease again. I settle back in to the fullness, peace and calm.

*Yes...Be still.*

I take it as a choice to *BE,* still - to stay alive. Done.

This resolution, this clarity, this choice shifts something inside me. I'm *beginning to feel my strength, my value, my capability, my nature, my potential, my power, my life.* Where birth feels like a passive default, choosing not to die feels like...life.

I rest here for a while, then stand up and walk home. Not fully aware of it yet, I've turned a corner. And slowly from within, a new life, a real life is beginning to surface.

*"Yesterday I was willing to die. Today I am willing to live."* - Van Jones

# 2

## ENOUGHNESS PERSPECTIVE

Funny, really, the idea of wanting death badly enough that it brought me to life. I've since found this experience of profound peace and inherent value can heal what I thought had been a permanently damaged self-regard and depressed life. Being able to tie that late night awakening to a *primal feeling* of worth, value, capability and possibility helped restore my humanity, my humility, my hope. My Enoughness.

So what is this word *Enoughness!?* What does it mean? Isn't it made up? Yes. I made it up. And I give it meaning. And it gives me meaning. It was the best name for the job. Like an arrow to a bullseye. Right on. And I suspect you get it. I don't really need to tell you what it means. You intuitively know what it means, what it feels like.

To me, Enoughness is a f*eeling, a perspective, a source to live well from.* Yes it's about being and feeling enough – enough for happiness, success and well-being. It doesn't just stop there, at your inner life. I also describe it as *a highly motivating personal equilibrium*. It applies to your outer experience in life as well. Centered. Balanced. Focused. A stance from which to lean into life rather than be blown over.

The literal definition from Webster's for 'equilibrium' is - *a state of mental or emotional balance (peace), being self-possessed, having presence of mind, calmness, and an evenness*.

In addition to an evenness, I define this particular personal equilibrium as a *state of being* that includes *remembering your inherent value so you can recognize what true fulfillment feels like to you and live a fully expressed life*. This is a powerful perspective from which to live a full and fulfilling life.

And it's a perspective either previously experienced or intuitively discovered. I believe it lies dormant in everyone. I've also experienced that it can be activated, fully developed and realized inside and out. It's not permanent. Yet it's a perpetual and powerful beginning to live from and return to.

It's like magic. Once developed, you can conjure Enoughness at will. And it can be experienced *independent of circumstances or history*. Best of all, it can eventually help you to consciously transform any unwanted circumstance into a wanted one.

Enoughness. Equilibrium. Evenness. If you've felt it once, you can feel it again. You can live in it and from it. You can do this right now. You can wisely and powerfully shape the very circumstances of your life *around this consciously chosen feeling and perspective.*

Anything is possible. I call this *living FROM Enoughness.*

Living *from* this state of Enoughness opens you up to vast inner resources (creativity, capability, intuition, imagination, potential, skill and talent) as well as the *natural will to wield those resources into a deeply fulfilling and fully expressed life.*

This manuscript takes you on the journey of Enoughness, mine and yours. It encourages you to discover and develop your own as I share mine. Enoughness is about the *art of fulfillment and full creative expression* that begins *within you*, not outside of you and not in someone else.

Through the process, what I've found is that the experience of Enoughness is *very creative.* And creativity is a great and empowering feeling for any human. It really is that vitalizing, motivating equilibrium. Your inner world and your outer experience can come together. There's a feeling of completion that leads to just getting down to creative business. Doing your duty. Feeling in tact and on track.

In this balance, the internal informs the external and the external informs the internal. It's a play, a dance between worlds rather than a battle. They are inter-dependent experiences. Heaven and earth belong together. It may not be easy at first but it can become your most natural state of being. You'll leave it and come back to it over and over, as I did. As I do.

And I can attest that one without the other, the inner without the outer, can quickly cause the dragon-chasing, ghost-riding, fear-mongering doubt and desperation that can bring only misery to life - as it did with mine. Well it's time for the exile of misery.

There's no right and perfect way to fully living a life. Yet I find Enoughness to be a great place to begin. And return. I find that it's a compass rather than a destination, a source rather than an effect, a beginning rather than an end. And I hope you can too.

*"Give me somewhere to stand and I will move the earth."* - Archimedes

# 3

## ENOUGHNESS CLAY

I wish I could say I stood up from that night in the park and shouted from the rooftops that I will live and live like never before! That didn't happen. Life isn't usually that pretty and perfect. It doesn't typically come with a Hollywood ending.

Instead, I needed time to let it sink in. I needed time to fumble around a bit. I needed time to slowly feel into again, to push it around, to feel this Enoughness *clay* in my hands. I needed time to explore how it feels, how to shape it and how to recreate it. Maybe later I could make this a way of life rather than a glorious but passing moment.

I eventually discovered that the liberation of Enoughness wasn't a one-time thing. It was exciting and encouraging that the *central experience* I felt in the park had remained. And it wasn't a ceiling. It wasn't a final destination. *Enoughness was a new beginning. It was the feeling of something central –*

*innocence, being restored.* And with practice, I learned to live in it.

The 2am epiphany I had wasn't a Messianic moment. It was a human one. It was revolutionary to me because it was a profound reminder that *the blueprint for value, fulfillment and a fully expressed life was already inside.* I no longer needed to look outside myself for my truest value and fulfillment. Now that I knew the blueprint was there, I could use it as a map, a compass. And I could pass it on.

This experience of Enoughness showed me a deep human desire to break free and live fully. I imagine the acorn breaking its own shell to become the oak has the same inherent desire. If you're human — and I guarantee you are, even if sometimes you don't feel like it — the experience of Enoughness is open to you as well.

# 4

## GOLDILOCKS FULFILLMENT

*Just be happy*, they say. Could you be more specific? How do I know when I'm happy? And it seems you're assuming I have the option to be happy and I choose to be otherwise. You're not being specific and you're not helping! Enoughness will get specific for you.

A fulfilling and expressed life is a happy life. Take for fun example the fable of Goldilocks and the Three Bears. In the story, Goldilocks — adventurer that she is — finds the cabin of the bears, enters, and tries out all the bowls of porridge, all the chairs, and finally, all the beds. Each time, she finds one that's *fulfilling* and just right - not too much, not too little.

Goldilocks' knows what she wants, goes after it and gets it. Her fulfillment compass, her self-value barometer, her *Enoughness* muscle is not yet twisted up from other people telling her what she can or can't do or who she can or can't be. She doesn't have that falsely manufactured, doubt-filled inner voice telling her she doesn't have what it takes to make her ideas a reality. She walks in her natural confidence and knows what it feels like to be fulfilled.

The driving inadequacy so many people feel of *settling for less while always wanting more* doesn't drive Goldilocks. She naturally wants what's *just right* for her and knows when she's fulfilled. To top it all off, she's able to find joy without the weight of shame or inadequacy telling her she doesn't deserve it.

Goldilocks lives with the natural confidence to know what she wants, go after it and feel fulfilled when she gets it. And in this cycle, she's has an everlasting, natural peace in her step. Her experience of finding day-to-day fulfillment isn't crippled by the toxic combination of painful self-doubt and chronic dissatisfaction.

The experience of *true* fulfillment, the kind only you know for yourself, is what brings you to Enoughness. You can, and should, trust yourself, especially when it comes to your own fulfillment. That's just wise. *Living from your fulfillment is the place where your inner Goldilocks can take a seemingly fairy tale experience and bring it to life.* It's having your cake and eating it too - or your porridge for that matter.

# 5

## KNIFE POINT

At 11 years old I survived a violent knifepoint attack. I'd ridden my bike to a nearby park for soccer practice. The park was very big. I was early, and there was no one around except for some kids playing at a far-off playground. I'd been to this park many times and was comfortable with the area. I decided to wait and lean on my bike until my coach and the other players showed up.

At one point, I looked back over my shoulder and saw a strange disheveled man coming towards me. He made me eerily uncomfortable but I didn't know why. I ignored the feeling. When I turned away again, he quickly tackled me from behind and knocked me to the ground. Within seconds he was sitting on my chest, holding what I remember to be a rusty knife blade to my throat, saying, *"Shut up. Don't scream or I'll f\*\*\*ing kill you."*

I think I screamed. I don't remember if I actually made any noise at first. The police later told me that sometimes, in panic a situation, the larynx gets extremely tight and even though you might be screaming, you're barely making a sound.

Soon enough though, I *heard* myself screaming and crying and felt myself wiggling, trying to get away. He held the knife tighter to my throat and repeated, *"If you move or make a another sound, I'll kill you."*

At that young age, I had no real concept yet of death or that my own life could end. But the fear and the terror I felt in my body told every ounce of me that this was a life-threatening attack.

He gave up on keeping my quiet, started moving slowly down my body and began pulling down my pants. Right then, paralyzed in fear, I shouted out, *"My Mom died yesterday!"* This wasn't true. It just popped out.

He stopped and seemed very agitated. As I continued struggling and trying to escape, he suddenly let go and just said *"You're crazy, kid."* Then he took off running.

Something about what I said scared him away. I don't care what it was, an angel or a smart remark, it worked. Crying and terrified, I got up, grabbed my bike and walked home.

I couldn't think, couldn't understand. When I got home, I told my parents what happened. The police came and took a report. They did their best to console me but ultimately there wasn't much they could do. And it was the best my family could do to be sensitive and supportive to me over the following months.

One of the hardest memories about this experience isn't just the terror in the park but how my four closest friends reacted to it - they didn't believe me (a common response to trauma). And after a few weeks, it was clear that the friendship was fading. One day on the playground at school, they gave me an envelope with a note in it. The note read *"We don't want to be friends anymore."*

There was no explanation. It happened so fast I didn't know what hit me. Needless to say, it sucked. The feelings of rejection and the sense of abandonment hit me hard for years to come.

The toughest part was spending the *next seven years* avoiding the notorious-four in the halls at school. I spent a lot of years hiding not just from the attack but from the kids in my own school! And from simply being myself. Insecurity grew exponentially as my voice laid stagnant for years. Expressing myself and seeking support meant rejection and disapproval.

I became ashamed. I became insecure. I became even more reclusive. I wasn't born that way. I learned it. The cool part is, *I've also unlearned it.* (Note it: with practice, you can unlearn repression, insecurity, fear, doubt and worry).

My attack and my subsequent behavior must have left my friends scared and confused to do such a thing. Either way, I was suddenly friendless in a very scary time of need. Alone and in the dark...

However, a couple days later, a kid named Dean (a schoolmate/teammate and now lifetime hero) saw me sitting alone outside and invited me to join him and his group of friends. I gladly accepted. And just like that I had a place to belong. Though the mark was made, at least I belonged somewhere. Dean and I were close friends for many years. I'll always be thankful for his noble invitation and his friendship.

I eventually found my way out of those dark hallways. It took many years to find my voice, my power and the freedom to be myself. I have Hollywood (and years of acting classes/therapy) to thank for that!

I can speak up and speak out now. I've earned my 'quiet' stripes. And it's ok to speak out. In fact, being expressed and expressive is a powerful contributor to the experience of Enoughness. Back then, I became scared to make a move or say a word, much less stand up and speak out for myself.

*The heart of Enoughness has become the fierce encouragement and the simple redemption of self-expression.*

With the strength of inherent worth and the capability of being fully expressed, you can come fully to life. There may be multiple misfortunes in life before redemption can be experienced. *But just one taste of it can guide you forever.*

Living to tell about the attack is a massive blessing. Living consciously and purposefully, honestly and openly again is the best thanks to give for a second chance. This kind of recovery carries with it a triumphant ending – a reclaimed life, a new beginning and a chance to grow again.

I'm here to support your own personal experience of Enoughness and a life beyond insecurity and adversity. I hope this message can be a part of your truest fulfillment, expression and success in life. It doesn't matter how many years have passed or how many years it takes - I believe a deeply fulfilling and fully expressed life is your (and my) destiny.

# 6

## FACING INSECURITY

It's easy to see there are an overwhelming number of people stuck, feeling insecure, inadequate, and just plain old not-enough. Having spent so much of my life there, inside and out, I can recognize it the many faces all around me.

It might show up in two ways; depressed, quiet, lowly human beings just trying to eek their way through life or overbearing control/power fanatics trying to own everything and everyone. Both are essentially fueled by a *chronic state of personal insecurity and not-enoughness.*

It seems this feeling shows up as *crippling self-doubt, depression and a deeply unfulfilled humanity.* It can be seen in the over-achieving billionaire, the marginalized voiceless many and everything in between. Insecurity has been something human beings have been trying to escape, control or destroy since the dawn of humanity. Insecurity, though it's a natural part of being a human animal, has been seen as a pariah or a mistake. *Enoughness taught me to look at insecurity from another angle.*

Even after standing strong on the foundation of Enoughness, my insecurity isn't going away. I can heal my history yet I'll never remove my humanity. For the human animal, insecurity is a constant. And as a constant, *it can be used as a guide.*

*Insecurity can be a messenger, not an enslaver.*

Insecurity could actually be the source and strength of humanity rather than the bane of it. I believe rather than making you feel inadequate it's simply *asking for your attention.* I believe it's meant not to get you stuck in a negative reaction but move you to *know yourself better, challenge your capabilities and develop your expressive self.* On a basic level, insecurity can shape your character and be a source of motivation.

The feeling of insecurity I felt as a kid when that man came creeping up behind me in the soccer park *was a hint and a warning.* It was telling me I was unsafe and preparing me to take fast action. I remember that feeling, that warning, viscerally even today. I took it then as a lack of confidence or strength, something I had to ignore or overcome. Today I take those messages as powerful nudges to pay attention. However, I don't take them to be the measure of my value or the definition of who I am.

Can you imagine if I continued to see this *inner nudge* as a negative character trait and decided to stifle, hide or ignore it? I can. It's the depressed, disconnected life I got stuck in!

A more useful stance is to work with those feelings, see them as *supportive* and then *choose how to live*. That's acting from wise discernment. Living a life of fear and paralyzing feelings of insecurity is not the only choice.

Living in and from Enoughness is another option for responding the feelings of insecurity. Enoughness becomes the priority, the starting point, which allows your feelings of insecurity, inadequacy and not-enoughness to sit in the back seat rather than drive the car.

It's possible to correct the course of paralyzing insecurity towards a life of motivating Enoughness, true fulfillment and a full creative expression. The perspective of Enoughness allows space for past hurt and pain. It allows space for flaring insecurity. And in that space, it reminds you of your original, inherent, valuable and capable nature, providing an atmosphere for empowered action.

Instead of insecurity having you feel like there's something wrong with you, it's a chance to know and grow yourself. There will always be the unknown inside and around you. It's not meant to make you insecure or keep you stuck in insecurity. A good friend of mine says it best, "Life's purpose is to grow and develop into our full selves. Insecurities actually help us develop. Insecurity is the way out of insecurity." – Dr. Angel Hall, PhD

Learning and growing into the unknown is extremely healthy and can actually be very entertaining. Think of the unknown *not as personal lack* but as endless opportunities to be *entertained and entertaining!* There's always something good in it. From Enoughness, feelings of insecurity can simply be empowering nudges to grow.

# 7

## NAMING ENOUGHNESS
## GUERRILLA CONTENTMENT

Though the epiphany in the park was profound, it was as temporary as a celebrity marriage. For months after, I was still in the thick of depression and decline. Frustrated and fed up, I went searching for that epiphany again.

I did what had helped before and what I was guided to do in that Los Angeles city park – I wept like a baby! And then I sat down and got really still. In the stillness, the peace and the strength from that night bubbled up. In the stillness, something began to shift. I didn't need to make big sweeping efforts. I had to let go of over-efforting, slow down and remember.

At this point in time, I didn't have a name for what I was recalling. I simply wanted to experience that sweet and natural feeling. Stillness helped me get clear enough to remember and to soak in the quiet relief again.

It was new. I had no name for it. And isn't funny how giving something a name makes it more real? So I asked for one. In meditation, in silence and stillness I asked, *"What is the name of the experience, the feeling I had?"* The word *Enoughness* popped in.

Similar to when my eardrum burst or blurting out random words that made my attacker run away on the soccer field, the word Enoughness *spontaneously* came to me. I'd not heard it or read it before. And even though it wasn't an actual word, it was a perfectly fitting name.

*Finding the name was a revelation.* I could almost begin to feel it at will once I named it. Or almost at will. With dedicated practice, I was building that ability. At the root of it was an origin, a source, a name.

I felt I could begin to create a whole life around it. The name granted me space and direction to explore this newfound state of being at my own pace. First it was about healing an injured soul and a depressed life. Later it became about *going beyond healing* into realizing what I was capable of – *true fulfillment and a fully expressed life.*

Naming it meant that what I unwittingly loved best about life, fulfillment and confident self-expression, are now less dependent on the outer world and more influenced by a chosen, nourishing inner state. I like to call this experience *guerrilla contentment* because it's like circumventing the process of happiness. And why not circumvent it?! It's not cheating; it's just purposefully fostering an empowering, experienced and consciously chosen feeling.

Naming a chosen feeling and life is claiming your birthright to it - I named it all *Enoughness.*

While typically "fulfillment" is based on external results, Enoughness means feeling a sense of fullness, completion and success regardless of externalities. It's knowing your inherent value that feeds and sustains true fulfillment. External fulfillment is nice as well. Enoughness is actually an empowering position for intentionally *shaping* and taking part in the externalities. And it's one to grow on. Giving it a name is the beginning.

Take a look at other names for what true fulfillment is and what it isn't.

*Webster's Dictionary:*

*ANTONYMS*

**Not-Enough:** Inadequate, incomplete, lacking, unequal, weak, barren, impotent, incapable, deficient, dissatisfactory.

*SYNONYMS*

**Enough:** Abundant, reached, attained, arrived, satisfied, ample, full, bountiful, sufficient, whole, complete, plentiful, able, capable, potent, full, strong, competent.

You can see (and feel) that words have a powerful effect. If you don't recognize what Enoughness means to you yet, I'm sure you can relate to feeling *satisfied, whole, able, strong, capable and/or competent.* And I'm sure you can also relate to words like incomplete, inadequate, lacking, weak, deficient, or defective. With Enoughness, I choose to relate to the former over the latter. How about you?

Enoughness, just the name, seeks to offer you the living *experience* behind all these wonderful synonyms. Take it on for yourself. Get used to using, and feeling the word. Contemplate it. Focus on it. Speak it out.

And take it all the way in by asking yourself *what does Enoughness mean to you?*

# Reasonable Inadequacy

For further clarity, I believe there *are* healthy levels of feeling 'inadequacy'. Reasonable inadequacy is what I call *having feelings of not-enoughness that can be reasonably based on current circumstances.* For example, being in an abusive relationship or a job that doesn't fit may be a circumstance that constantly contributes to feelings of not-enoughness. These are hints towards a needed change. Take the hint; yet take it from encouragement rather than discouragement.

# Unreasonable Inadequacy

Unreasonable inadequacy is having feelings of not-enoughness that are *unreasonably* based on your general personal value and worth regardless of (current or past) circumstances. Simultaneously, these could be feelings that seem to dictate behavior and decision-making while ultimately stifling your growth. *Not to mention leaving you forever discontent!* These feelings help to create circumstances that become cohorts to feelings of unreasonable inadequacy in your life.

What I've found is that life can be an experience of both. And both can be brought into balance with the right tools in hand. The experience of Enoughness can be a very useful and accessible practice for finding this balance. The practice, (shared later in this book) as well as the names and synonyms listed above, helps *point the way* to true fulfillment and a fully expressed life.

# 8

## LIVING
## A FULLY EXPRESSED LIFE
## ACTING IT OUT

Though after 10 years of acting I hadn't found commercial success, I'd found something else – *creativity*. And now, I fervently believe the life-blood of human happiness is to be fully, creatively and powerfully expressed in life and work, in words and action.

The world of acting in Los Angeles and NYC gave me a safe haven to find the ever-so-valuable voice, body and spirit of my creative self-expression. The many classes, plays and independent films I was a part of not only invited me be creative, it begged it of me. What a gift.

Acting helped me find myself by losing myself over and over again in characters, roles and stories. By stretching into the behaviors, thoughts and words of other characters, I found a mirror to myself. After all and in the end, it wasn't the 'character' being and doing all these things; it was my own self. It was my own thoughts, feelings, perceptions, understanding and eclectic expressions. The back and forth of blending character-study with self-study shaped my entire life becoming a creative self-expression.

And this isn't just expression for the sake of expression (which has it's place). This is the *art* of creative expression. It's a healing art. It's about discovering a personal authenticity that comes only from including yourself in the creative experience.

It's not about a show. Well it's not just about a show. It's about passing on an experience. And the most powerful way to do that is to be actually having the experience *yourself* while sharing it with others.

That equals authenticity. And it equals vulnerability. Creative expression needs to be connected to meaning that you personally find and define within. That's showing others who you are, how you feel and what you think. I used to think being vulnerable meant being weak. Can you relate? Man or woman, I'm sure you can. Now I see it simply points towards your own unique way of being and doing things. And that needs a place in the world. Don't you think?

It's frightening at first. Then it becomes a genuine human accomplishment. It's empowering and rewarding in itself.

And it needs to be genuine and authentic if it's going to be rewarding to an audience. In order to give an audience a powerful acting performance, I had to find a way *every time* to be authentic. It became my obsession to find authenticity in every performance, character and story. It allowed me to flush up all the crap from my life and use it for something good. And that was healing as much as it was creative. Maybe healing and creativity are the same thing.

Through acting, I found the pure and intrinsic joy of authentic and creative self-expression. Not to say the joy wasn't often matched by sorrow, sadness and pain. Many times authenticity asked that I look at the light and the dark parts of myself and of life. It was always worth it. And as long as I kept with that intrinsic experience, authenticity was assured and satisfying every time.

Even as I've formally studied business, spirituality and consciousness, I attribute my greatest growth, joy, wonder and self-discovery to the art and craft of acting. I wasn't a natural. On stage in front of audiences or in front of a camera, I had to learn how to let go of my insecurities and just go for it. Repeatedly putting myself through this painful experience was ultimately the most rewarding (and somewhat masochistic) thing I could've done.

I grew up a shy and uncomfortable-in-my-skin kind of kid. Yet even in my itchy discomfort, I still had the audacity to feel like there was something magic far beyond the itch. I believed, in a deeply romantic way, that there had to be something beyond an unfulfilling, unexpressed and lackluster life. I now believe an expressed life is not only a gift but a spiritual mandate.

Acting, as creative self expression, brought me to life. It helped me practice feeling seen, present and even sometimes strong in my own skin. It helped me break through personal 'shells' of disbelief that kept me quiet for too long. Because of my long-time discomfort and self-doubt, it took years of acting classes and practice to just stand up and talk in front of other people. When I did, it was a temporary cure for all the maladies of life. One of my greatest challenges was playing a crazy, dangerous, out of control character in a three-hour dramatic play.

I was the lead role in Sam Shepard's 'A Lie of the Mind', at a small playhouse in Los Angeles, CA. (Sam Shepard is known for writing plays that are gut wrenching, intensely dramatic, and highly emotional). This one happened to be three hours long! It was just the right invitation for a shy, pensive guy trying to break free from his own chains.

I played the central male character, Jake, who's a volatile and violent mess. And for a natural introvert, it took real work to get there! Here's a description of the play from Wikipedia.

> Told in three acts set in the gritty American West, the (play) alternates between two families after a severe incident of spousal abuse leaves all their lives altered until the final collision at an isolated cabin. The two families...are connected by the marriage of Jake and Beth, whose betting and subsequent hospitalization at the hands of Jake initiates the beginning of the play. Exploring familier dysfonction and the nature of love, the play follows Jake as he searches for meaning after Beth, and her familier, struggle with Beth's brain damage.

The play opens with Jake on the street at night, crying and yelling into a payphone to his brother right after having beaten his wife, Beth, unconscious. As the lights came up to start the play, I'm already at full speed. I'm crying and yelling and banging the earpiece of the phone of a street-side phone booth. I'm trying to get my brother's help and attention on the other side of the line.

I was so hyped up I yanked the fake silver phone cord out of the phone booth! I quickly noticed the cord was loose, fixed it fast and continued on with the frantic conversation. We continued on with the rest of the scene. Soon enough, the lights went out. The first act was complete. Well done. It was a serious high. The rest of the play went off without a hitch and we had a great run of the play for the next few weeks.

Acting was foundational in learning the intrinsic value of play, exploration and creative self-expression. As an actor, it was about building the character for a creative project. *Now it's about building the container for a creative life.*

It's in you too - the call to be fully creatively expressed. True fulfillment and full creative expression are at the heart of Enoughness. Sometimes it takes pushing through fear to find your authentic voice. Though it can be uncomfortable and sometimes painful, breaking through your fears opens you up to a *whole,* new world.

# 9

## THE SEMI-SCIENCE OF ENOUGHNESS

This has been a story about a depressed life redeemed by the pure yet spontaneous experience of inherent value transforming into true fulfillment and a fully expressed life. I've discovered there's also a *semi-science* behind the *story* of Enoughness. Hopefully, the two together explain the *heart* of it. Like the practice, the semi-science of Enoughness can help you find, describe and experience it.

Bruce Lipton is an American developmental biologist who is best known for promoting the idea that genes and DNA can be powerfully influenced by a person's beliefs. One of his most popular books, *The Biology of Belief*, says:

> *If humans were to model the lifestyle displayed by healthy communities of cells, our societies and our planet would be more peaceful and vital. Creating such a peaceful community is a challenge because every person*

*perceives the world differently. So essentially, there are (seven billion) versions of reality on this planet, each perceiving its own truth. As the population grows, they are bumping up against each other.*

*Cells faced a similar challenge in early evolution. Shortly after the earth was formed, single-celled organisms rapidly evolved. Thousands of variations of unicellular bacteria, algae, yeast and protozoa, each with varying levels of awareness, appeared over the next three and a half billion years. It is probable that like us, those single-celled organisms began to multiply seemingly out of control and to over populate their environment. They began to bump up against each other and wonder, will there be enough for me?*

*It must have been scary for them, too. With that new, enforced closeness and the consequent change in their environment, they searched for an effective response to their pressures. Those pressures led to a new and glorious era in evolution, in which single cells joined together in altruistic multi-cellular communities. The end result was humans, at or near the top of the evolutionary ladder.*

Pioneering new territory has always come with challenges to grow, stabilize and sustain it. This is especially true when pioneering *inner territory!* After all, it's harder to see in there.

# Enoughness

Feeling the squeeze of not-enoughness, inadequacy and insecurity may seem like a barrier to realizing true fulfillment in life. Yet like Bruce Lipton's statement suggests, science might say these are actually the *perfect conditions* for the next evolution of your and humanities fulfillment, creativity and happiness. I know it's been true for me.

There are many great scientists and philosophers that describe gateways to activating human potential, evolution and full happy actualization. One of those *mind-scientists* is American psychologist Abraham Maslow. In his best-selling book, *Toward a Psychology of Being*, the experience of Enoughness would likely be filed under what he calls a *Peak Experience*.

# 10

## THE PEAK EXPERIENCE

Abraham Maslow is a well-respected and pioneering psychologist from the mid-20ᵗʰ Century. He is well known for his model of the *hierarchy of human needs*, a model he designed in order to point to, enliven, and encourage humans to realize their full potential.

Abraham Maslow's theories on human motivation, *optimal fulfillment and self-actualization* are similar to the philosophy of Enoughness. His frameworks are helpful in breaking down and digesting this way of living. His central philosophy focuses on the importance of growing and evolving into your highest potentials and becoming fully self-actualized.

It always feels so good, better than almost any other feeling you could have, being self-actualized. I suppose I call it self-expressed. I imagine it's what a flower feels when it reaches its petals open to the sky and fully blooms. What a great stretch!

One of the wise qualities of Maslow's work was to focus on health and well-being. For instance, in one of his studies, instead of focusing on malady and disease, Maslow studied the healthiest 1% of the college student population. He said, *"The study of crippled, stunted, immature and unhealthy specimens can only yield a cripple psychology and a cripple philosophy."* His work was meant to bring out the best in people. And the same is true of the purpose and function of living from Enoughness rather than not-enoughness.

Maslow describes a concept he calls *meta-motivation*, or the *"motivation of people who are self-actualized and striving beyond the scope of their basic needs to reach and fulfill their inherent ultimate potential...What we can be, we must be."* This is also the aim of living a life from Enoughness.

## Meta-Motivation

Maslow states that in meta-motivation, or motivation beyond basic needs, *"People are spontaneous and free to be themselves, while exploring their ultimate potentials and creating a fulfilled life."* Ultimate potential is *inherent potential.* Like Inherent Value, your potentials are born automatically within you, given to you freely, and available for your conscious development and enjoyment.

52

# Characteristics of Self-Actualizers

In reading Maslow, I discovered the illuminating experience I had at 2am in the park was similar to what Maslow calls a *Peak Experience*. Maslow describes this experience as one of the elements of self-actualization. *"A **self-actualizer** is a person who is living creatively and fully using his or her creative potentials."* Imagine also a self-actualizer as someone who feels their inherent worth and value, feels deep fulfillment often and lives fully, creatively expressed.

In his studies, Maslow found that self-actualizers share these similarities:

> *Efficient perceptions of reality.* Self-actualizers are able to judge situations correctly and honestly. They are very sensitive to the fake and dishonest, and are free to see reality 'as it is'.

> *Comfortable acceptance of self, others, nature.* Self-actualizers accept their own human nature with all its flaws. The shortcomings of others and the contradictions of the human condition are accepted with humor and tolerance.

> *Spontaneity.* Self-actualizers extend personal creativity into everyday activities. Actualizers

53

tend to be unusually alive, engaged, and spontaneous.

➢ *Task centering.* Self-actualizers have a mission to fulfill in life or some task or problem 'beyond' themselves to pursue.

➢ *Autonomy.* Self-actualizers are free from reliance on external authorities or other people. They tend to be resourceful and independent.

➢ *Continued freshness of appreciation.* The self-actualizer seems to constantly renew appreciation of life's basic goods. A sunset or a flower will be experienced as intensely time after time as it was at first. There's an "innocence of vision", like that of an artist or child.

➢ *Fellowship with humanity.* Self-actualizers have a deep identification with others and the human situation in general.

➢ *Profound interpersonal relationships.* The interpersonal relationships of self-actualizers are marked by deep loving bonds.

➢ *Comfort with solitude.* Despite their satisfying relationships with others, self-actualizing persons value solitude and are comfortable being alone.

➤ *Non-hostile sense of humor.* This refers to the wonderful capacity to laugh at oneself. It also describes the kind of humor of a man like Abraham Lincoln. Lincoln probably never made a joke that hurt anybody. His wry comments were gentle prodding's of human shortcomings.

➤ ***PEAK EXPERIENCES.*** *Self-actualizers report the frequent occurrence of peak experiences (temporary moments of self-actualization). These occasions were marked by feelings of ecstasy, harmony, and deep meaning. Self-actualizers reported feeling at one with the universe, stronger and calmer than ever before, filled with light, beautiful and good, and so forth.*

Wow. What perfect and poetic descriptions, names and qualities of life. Qualities of experience. Qualities of a possible and researched experience. Just reading them feels good. Possibility always feels good. And I highlight *Peak Experience* because it's a possibility I can attest to. It clearly reflects my own 2am illuminating city park experience I later named Enoughness.

Because Maslow also gave this deep activating fulfillment a name (self-actualization), it dramatically humanizes it. Right? It helps prove that you and I can actually have the experience. It's not just theory. Maslow has pointed out that there's a *science* in discovering and living from this real way of life. My hope is to share the *art* of optimal fulfillment through the experience and practice of Enoughness.

*"In summary, self-actualizers feel finally themselves - secure, not anxious, accepted, loved, loving, and alive. Certainly living a fulfilling life!"* –Abraham Maslow

# 11

## IN THE FLOW

Mihaly Csikszentmihalyi is another *mind-scientist* in this study of human fulfillment. His popular book *Flow* describes an "Optimal Experience" or "Being in the Flow." His book talks about peak *performance* (rather than experience) or a state of *doing* rather than a state of being as with Enoughness. His theory is applied to a specialized *activity* with certain parameters that yield the experience of being in the 'flow'. Athletes and musicians are typical contexts for the flow-state, a state that hints at the experience of Enoughness.

Wikipedia describes Mihaly as *"A Hungarian psychology professor who now teaches at Claremont Graduate University. He is noted for his work in the study of happiness and creativity and is best known as the architect of the notion of flow and for his years of research and writing on the topic. He is the author of many books and over 120 articles or book chapters. Martin Seligman, former president of the American Psychological Association, described Csikszentmihalyi as the world's leading researcher on positive psychology.*

Csikszentmihalyi once said *"Repression is not the way to virtue. When people restrain themselves out of fear, their lives are by necessity diminished. Only through freely chosen discipline can life be enjoyed and still kept within the bounds of reason."*

Csikszentimihalyi also says *"In Confucian China, in ancient Sparta, in Republican Rome, in the early Pilgrim settlements of New England, and among the British upper classes of the Victorian era, people were held responsible for keeping a tight rein on their emotions. Anyone who indulged in self-pity, who let instinct rather than reflection dictate actions, forfeited the right to be accepted as a member of the community.*

*In other historical periods, such as the one in which we are now living, the ability to control oneself is not held in high esteem. People who attempt it are thought to be faintly ridiculous, 'uptight' or not quite 'with it'. But whatever the dictates of fashion, it seems that those who take the trouble to gain mastery over what happens in consciousness do live a happier life."*

If living a happy, full and creative life is important to you, then living in and from Enoughness is definitely 'with it'. *Enoughness seeks to land you right smack between having too much or too little control of yourself and your life.* What a beautiful balance. My hope is that by continuing to focus on Enoughness that you (and I) experience it more often, personally and collectively. Living from Enoughness, then, might even be synonymous with being cool! Yes it's true.

In his book, *Flow: The Psychology of Optimal Experience*, Mihaly describes how people are happiest when they're in a particular state of flow. *"Flow is a state of concentration or complete absorption with the activity at hand and the situation. It is a state in which people are so involved in an activity that nothing else seems to matter. The idea of flow is identical to the feeling of being in the zone or in the groove. The flow state is an optimal state of intrinsic motivation, where the person is fully immersed in what they are doing. This is a feeling everyone has at times, characterized by a feeling of great absorption, engagement, fulfillment, and skill—and during which temporal concerns (time, food, ego-self, etc.) are typically ignored."*

In reading Mihaly's book, I focused on ideas that were similar to the experience of Enoughness. Mihay's *flow* experience (or peak *performance)* is more centrally focused on a particular feeling during a specific *activity or task*. It relates more to a state of *doing*. The *peak experience* as Maslow puts it, tilts more towards a state of *being*. For example, peak performance is most experienced by athletes or musicians being in the "zone" *during performance*. Enoughness and the *peak experience* are experiential and relate to an overall state of *being or feeling*.

## Mihaly on Flow:

*"In reality, to achieve such an ordered mental condition is not as easy as it sounds. Contrary to what we tend to assume, the normal state of the mind is chaos…when we are left alone, with no demands on attention, the basic disorder of the mind reveals itself. With nothing to do, it begins to follow random patterns, usually stopping to consider something painful or disturbing.*

*Unless a person knows how to give order to his or her thoughts, attention will be attracted to whatever is most problematic at the moment: it will focus on some real or imaginary pain, on recent grudges or long-term frustrations. Entropy is the normal state of consciousness, a condition that is neither useful nor enjoyable…To avoid this condition, people are naturally eager to fill their minds with whatever information is readily available, as long as it distracts attention from turning inward and dwelling on negative feelings. This explains why such a huge proportion of time is invested in watching television, despite the fact that it is very rarely enjoyed.*

*Compared to other sources of stimulation, like reading, talking to other people, or working on a hobby, TV can provide continuous and easily accessible information that will structure the viewers attention, at a very low cost in terms of the psychic energy that needs to be invested...The better route for **avoiding chaos in consciousness**, of course, is through habits that give control over mental processes to the individual, rather than to some external source of stimulation, such as the programs of network TV." (Emphasis mine)*

Developing and practicing Enoughness allows you a personal claim to fulfillment. It's a *conscious focus* that can be a healthy *focal point* that can help bring order to the naturally chaotic mind. You can return to this state of mind/being by choice throughout your daily living and practice. It's a simple way to bring order to chaos and manage your life and work from an empowered command of your attention. Enoughness becomes, as Mihaly calls it, a *"chosen discipline."*

# 12

## ENOUGHNESS, SUCCESS & THE MEANTIME

What is success? That's a whole other book. In this book, it's remembering your inherent value, finding true fulfillment, and living a fully expressed life. Success is an experience rather than a result. And of course, in that experience, beneficial results are part of it. After all, *Enoughness is not merely a soft state of survival!* Results are good.

When you can create the feeling of success within, you'll no longer depend on the outer world to provide it for you. You'll provide it for yourself. And the world will shape itself around your inner-living success. Doesn't that just sound right? Don't take my word for it. Or do. Either way, find out for yourself. Yet I can tell you that the ability to create within you a desired experience at will, frees you from the desperation, doubt and depression that come with being externally dependent on it. Enoughness is a chosen feeling. And it can banish the unwanted ones.

There seems to be a gap between failure and success. To close that gap, try looking at them as two sides of the same coin, or two pair of binoculars looking at the same vision. You can do all the work and preparation you want. But if you're starting from the 'failure' perspective, failure will be your destiny. Catching and developing a feeling is a sure way to change and rightly align your perspective. And your destiny.

Enoughness refers to an equilibrium - *a peak experience* that includes feelings of deep fulfillment and full creative expression. This is the *feel* of success. This is the kind of experience you want to develop from the inside out. It takes practice.

And it's the space *between* opportunities where real success is built. And practiced. After all, there could be large gaps between opportunities. *So what do you do in the meantime?*

Great question. How's this for an answer? – Using a practice, harness and conjure the feeling of fulfillment until it takes over your circumstances as well as your heart. Then call that success and see what happens.

The practice of *fostering a feeling* is a big help for those in-between spaces. Practice helps you stay ready, focused, prepared, available and fresh when those opportunities for success show up. They grow you into readiness, like a cocoon for a caterpillar to become a butterfly.

You're creating the atmosphere of success within yourself until it collides with the outward and full expression of it. Full creative expression means having an idea as well as the ability and opportunity to put it into viable and sharable action.

Enoughness and the peak experience are about *what you do before, until and during success.* The practice is the way or the formula to bridge the gap between feeling and reality. The practice fills the gaps leading to sustainable success by being prepared. Otherwise, when those sweet peak experiences and successes do show up, they're only temporary and elusive moments. And where's the success in that?

# 13

## THE PRACTICE OF ENOUGHNESS
## ENOUGHNESS EMERGES

*"Our main task is to discover and fulfill our deep innate potential, much as the acorn contains the potential to become the oak, or the caterpillar to become the butterfly."* – Carl Jung

Enoughness is both a lifelong journey and a chosen destination. It's a place to move from and reside in. With practice, Enoughness emerges.

The Practice of Enoughness aims to *create the condition* for your natural gifts, talents and potentials to be developed and fully expressed. It's a guide rather than a rule. Use it to discover your own equilibrium.

I studied the art, craft and business of acting intensely for 10 years. And along the way, my teachers would say - *"Learn it and let it go."* I was baffled at first. Why learn it at all if I'm only in the end going to let it all go? The idea behind that thinking is that practicing, embracing and letting go means *allowing what remains to naturally emerge.* And what naturally emerges is you and yours. It's a practice in pulling out your own core self and strength so you own it. The practice I've created is meant only to bring you your own definition and experience of lasting fulfillment.

Without rehearsal in acting, only short bursts of natural ability tend to show up. It's just beginners luck. It takes intention and practice to make it consistent and reliable art. Without a conscious practice in fulfillment, only a half life is lived, not a full one.

*It's consistent practice that gives birth to a chosen and sustainable experience.* It's about creating your circumstances, your life as you see fit. Practice makes the world go 'round. It gives you tools to shape your way when you need it, want it or just feel like being artful in life. With practice, the tools are always there at some level, helping your life experience be that much more reliable, enjoyable and fulfilling.

For greater clarity and ease, the Practice of Enoughness is broken into three parts:

# The Practice of Enoughness

*Finding Peace*

*Fostering a Feeling*

*Right Action & Achievement*

*Finding Peace is:*

Recognizing your inherent value, independent of your history, successes or failures. Experiencing inner calm and quiet. Being comfortable in your own skin. Being grounded, present, open and available. Feeling whole, worthy and connected.

*Fostering a Feeling is:*

Feeling capable, creative, valuable, inspired and alive. Feeling purposeful and engaged. Discovering, shaping, expressing and sharing your most unique talents, gifts and abilities.

*Right Action & Achievement is:*

Acting on consciously chosen goals that are aligned with your inner value, talents and abilities. Using inner peace, talent, capability and measurable action to achieve desired results.

# Response-Ability

Before the practice begins, take a look at the word *responsibility*. Living in and practicing Enoughness takes *Response-Ability*. Your truest peace and creativity lives *in the space between stimulus and response*. Growing that space means strengthening your ability and choice to *respond rather than react*. The opposite of this ability is an unconscious, choice-less, disempowered *reactivity*.

Though the animal survival reaction of fight/flight/freeze is meant to keep you out of the mouth of saber tooth tigers, *it's not meant to inspire your entire life*. Enoughness, fulfillment, self-expression; creativity, talent, capability; empowerment and chosen action - *these* are qualities that are lifetime inspirations.

Dr. Rev. Michael Beckwith, founder of the *Agape International Spiritual Center* describes response-ability, or the ability to respond as *"Our ability to think, live, create and have your well-being independent of circumstances."* You can see how this aids in your ability to *choose* deep fulfillment and a fully expressed life.

Response-ability allows you to go beyond your adversities, beyond your history and beyond your circumstances to live the life you imagine. And *destiny speaks through imagination.*

As you find yourself continually *imagining* a truly fulfilling and fully expressed life, you're not just dreaming. Consider it your *destiny* speaking to you *through* imagination.

Living in and from Enoughness supports your destiny to be fulfilled and expressed, just like the acorn is meant to fulfill and express itself as the oak tree. Your destiny and imagination are cohorts to the experience of Enoughness.

# The 6 Life-Energy Buckets

Let me first introduce the six categories of life in which to practice Enoughness. You'll use them as reference guides throughout the entire practice. Imagine them as *fulfillment buckets that need balance*, that need to be rightly filled with your attention, energy and action.

*1. Life's Work*

Developing fulfillment in your work life. This includes many or all of the following qualities: *purposeful, engaging and soul-fulfilling work; financially rewarding, strongly engages your gifts and talents and provides appropriate recognition;*

provides room for growth and learning, inspiring challenges, creativity, vision and meaning; aligns with values, allows time to develop and implement new ideas, and has a clear social benefit. (This area can also include the awesome life's work of raising children full time).

## 2. Self-Care, Personal Growth & Spiritual Development

*Self-Care* includes *scheduled downtime and getaways, kind and supportive self-talk, a nurturing and encouraging Personal Ecosystem (described later in Fostering a Feeling); reading and writing for fun, healthy and engaging lifestyle habits in organic nutrition and stress and energy management practices like exercise, meditation, stillness and yoga practices.*

*Personal Growth* includes *attending workshops or educational events, reading and writing for growth, having a creative outlet; volunteering, traveling and exploring higher education.*

*Spiritual Development* includes *inspiring and consistent spiritual and devotional practice in prayer, meditation/stillness practice, fellowship and tithing.*

## 3. Financial Wellness

Developing fulfillment in your financial life. This includes many or all of the following qualities: *on-time bill payments, management of assets and money flow, creating strategy-*

driven savings and investment plans; insurance, estate planning, and long-term care; goals in increasing salary and income streams, contributing to charities and spiritual tithing.

## 4. Intimate Relationship (includes children)

Developing fulfillment in your current or wanted intimate relationship (includes children). This includes many or all of the following qualities: *intimacy, quality, enjoyment and inspiration; shared communication, agreements, independence and definitions.*

## 5. Immediate Family

Developing fulfillment in your relationship to your immediate family. This includes many or all of the following qualities: *consistent communication, quality, enjoyment, contribution and setting appropriate boundaries with your parents, stepparents, grandparents, siblings, extended family, in-laws.*

## 6. Social Life

Developing fulfillment in your social life. This includes many or all of the following qualities: *having fun for no reason, conscious and healthy friendships, shared recreation, events and celebration! This area also includes a social benefit to the planet and others, such as volunteering, recycling/reusing, and consistency in contributing to social good.*

# 14

## PRACTICES FOR FINDING PEACE

Inner peace, as I felt it in that pure breakthrough moment at 2am, is a deep feeling of your inherent value, wholeness, calm and connectedness. Enoughness, as dynamic inner peace, *technically begins here.*

Inner peace can be accomplished without having substantial outer resources. Many sages and saints show us this truth. Moreover, cultures in third world countries that are *stark in resources yet rich in smiling faces* are proof enough. At the same time, the ability to creatively *materialize* this inner life into your outer experience is the very process of shaping your destiny. Finding peace while living in and from it today determines how you shape and experience your tomorrow.

The practices for Finding Peace in this model include *Being Still and Knowing Your Inherent Value.*

# I. The Practice of BEING STILL

*"In the context of a meditative way of life, doing nothing can be experienced as the non-movement of sitting meditation, as a form of mental surrender, as effortless performance, intuitive action, open receptivity to constantly changing circumstances or at its peak as **an experience of immanent completeness without anything to be done and nothing to be sought after.**" (Emphasis added)* - Dr. Michelle K. Nielsen

Practicing Stillness simply allows you to take a break from the constant stimulation all around you. It's a time to draw within and find as much sweet value in your own inner life as your outer one. It allows you to take a moment to find, feel and harness your peace.

# 3 Benefits of Stillness

1. Stillness can help to shuffle off chaotic energy & release stress.
2. Stillness can create space for better decision-making & intentional action.
3. Stillness can help to reset your natural pace and conserve energy for deeper day-to-day fulfillment.

# Comparing Meditation & Stillness

I began to practice meditation in my late twenties. Basically my life *sucked!* I needed to find my way out of the forest of darkness and depression. Meditation helped me the most.

I started with a general slow breathing meditation. I'd sit in quiet with my eyes closed 'watching' my breath come in and out. It allowed me to *stop time* in short bursts, be with myself and simply relax. In that relaxation I could better see where I was in my life, where I was going and how I wanted to feel along the way. I then became interested in a more formal meditation. I learned and started practicing Transcendental Mediation (TM) twice a day for many years. Later, I explored the Bhakti yoga tradition of chanting mantras (as well as other practices) as another form of meditation and devotion, connecting with my center, my source and the Divine.

After all these years and methods of practicing (and with the powerful *nudge* from my 2am epiphany) the *calming stillness in these practices stood out the most.* I've focused on the *stillness* to create a simplified form of meditation.

The essential benefits remain the same including deep rest, connection, calm, peace, coherence and clarity.

# 4 Steps to Stillness

*"In stillness the world is restored."* - Lao Tzu

Breathe naturally and sit as *still* as humanly possible with every ounce of your body and being. Do this for a *consistent* and specific amount of time. Enjoy the calm. You're done.

I don't mean to over-simplify it. Yes I do. Simplicity is one thing. Finding a degree of *enjoyment* is another and it's actually a very good measure of doing it 'right.' Whether you're feeling light or heavy, happy or sad, up or down, you can always enjoy the simplicity of taking time to just *be still*.

In your practice, play like a child. Be as *still* as you've *ever ever ever* been. When you're mind races, and it will, it means you've subtly lost the easy focus of being still so you can instead think about groceries. Gently bring your focus back to being absolutely still. The groceries will be fine.

As you find your attention wandering or your mind racing, that's ok and absolutely normal! In fact, don't fight it. Why fight normal? If you can't beat 'em, join 'em! After all, the world, your body and your mind will always be in motion to some degree, no matter how still you become. Let go of the idea of stopping your mind. Practicing Stillness is like sitting in the middle of a river enjoying the flow without being swept away. It's a refreshing practice when you get used to it!

If you're mind races, go with it for a few moments. *Think think think!* Conclude your thought. Itch that mental scratch. Then gently and repeatedly bring your attention back to the focus and calm of *ultra-stillness.*

1.   Set <u>time of day and length</u> of practice

I recommend starting in the morning as soon as you wake up. If you'd like, brush your teeth, use the bathroom, take a shower, salute the sun and have a glass of water. (Try to do this on a fairly empty stomach; it's easier on the body/mind). Morning is recommended so you're starting your day from center but any time of day is better than none!

Start with 10 minutes daily for a month. Then work up to 20 minutes daily, forever and ever. Whatever it is, choose the time before beginning. Peek at the time or set a timer to know when you're complete. (Eventually, doing this two times a day, 10 or 20 minutes in the morning and 10 or 20 minutes in the evening, creates powerful long-term results).

2.   Sit in a dignified <u>posture</u> (tension-free and poised)

Sit in a cross-legged pose on the ground or on a pillow. If you'd rather, sit in a chair in cross-legged pose or keep your feet on the ground. Hands can be touching (or not) and resting naturally in your lap. Gently close your eyes. Take three deep belly breaths, all the way in and all the way out through the nose.

3.  Get *present, connected & grounded*.

Getting present, connected and grounded allows your nervous system and your brain to settle.

a. *Get present* by saying to yourself – *"Right here and right no - I let go of everything that's come before this moment. I let go of everything that may come after this moment. So I can be fully present, engaged and alive in this moment."*

b. *Get connected* to your body by using *"I'm Aware"* statements for two of your senses:

*Hearing*: Notice (to yourself) three things you're hearing. (i.e. I'm aware of hearing the sound of a jet engine, I'm aware of hearing the birds singing outside my window, I'm aware of the quiet in the room).

*Feeling*: Notice (to yourself) three things you're feeling. (i.e. I'm aware of feeling my heart beat, I'm aware of feeling the temperature of the room on my skin, I'm aware of feeling my sit-bones on the chair/pillow/floor).

c. *Get grounded* by releasing tension. Do a brief body scan from foot to head. Start by relaxing the arches of your feet, then your legs, hips, pelvis, belly, lower back, chest, shoulders, neck, throat, face, eyes, jaw and tongue; and finally, *gently soften your brain.* (Softening your brain starts first by relaxing your eyes and just behind your eyes. Then feel your brain releasing strain and tension while almost expanding in your cranium). *Tongue Note:* The best 'posture' for your tongue is basically NOT stuck to the roof of your mouth. Instead, drop and relax your tongue. Then lightly place the tip of your tongue just behind your two front teeth while relaxing the rest of it. This helps keep the connection between your body and brain.

## 4. *Be STILL*

You're time, place and posture are set. You've gotten present, connected and grounded. The first three steps may take a minute or two. *Now - be still* for the remainder of the 10 minutes (or the allotted time).

Gently focus on being *as still as a statue* with your body, mind and energy. Keep it simple. Play with it. Slow your breathing down at first to get the feel of it ultra-stillness. If you need to, take a deep breath and wiggle a bit. Then breathe naturally and be very still. Pretend as though you're turning yourself invisible to the world around you. Be so still that all you feel is your gentle breathing and heart beating. Very natural. In this *intentional stillness*, you're consciously bringing your mind, your body, your energy and your attention into coherence. *This coherence is true peace.*

Again, if your mind races or thoughts pull your attention away, that's ok. If you feel like moving and making an adjustment to your posture at anytime, do it. The back and forth is natural and it reflects the general nature of life (oceanic tides, breathing in and out, sun/moon orbits, etc). So embrace it. Notice the difference between movement and stillness. This contrast will actually help you more distinctly feel the benefits of being still.

When you've reached your time limit, take three deep belly breaths all the way in and all the way out through the nose. Enjoy this moment too. Let your body completely relax (lay all the way on the ground if you like) for a few moments and absorb the benefits. To end, wiggle your toes, gently stretch your arms up and out, breathe fully, and *very slowly,* open your eyes. *Nicely done.*

One more thing - I highly recommend adding *60-Seconds of Stillness* into your day. Once you've got the above practice down, sprinkle it across your waking hours. You'll love the relief and the opening you get from this brief stop. At your desk, on the bus or wherever you are (definitely not driving!), sit back and enjoy a refreshing minute of stillness.

*Secret – Bringing Stillness into Motion*

One of the greatest benefits and secrets of a successful Stillness Practice is bringing that stillness into motion. Do your best to extend the stillness, clarity and coherence of your mind, body and soul out into your day. *First comes the stillness and then comes the slow translation of that stillness into your every movement.*

Take your time coming out of the practice. Gracefully blend the moments of stillness into motion over and over, every time you practice. Bring this calm poised energy into your life. I think you'll find an increased sense of peace and poise comes to the surface.

## More Benefits...

1. Relieves stress & anxiety - Nurtures inner peace & joyfulness
2. Improves awareness, concentration & memory - Grounds & connects with intuition
3. Better processing of thoughts & feelings - Nurtures restfulness and calm
4. Contributes to mental clarity & sustained energy
5. Provides space for you to get out of your own way!

PS- You may fall asleep during the first few weeks or so of your Stillness Practice. Let yourself. I've fallen asleep plenty of times in my practice, at least for part of it. It's a good sign. You're getting deep rest and that's one of the main points of this kind of practice. Eventually, you'll be getting adequate rest and rejuvenation from a *consistent* practice that the inclination to fall asleep will likely fade naturally. Keep going. Be consistent. Enjoy.


# 11. The Practice of KNOWING YOUR INHERENT VALUE

*"Our worth is intrinsic to who we are, depending on nothing extrinsic, whether it be achievement, race, gender or whatever else."* – Archbishop Desmond Tutu

The definition of *inherent* is *"A quality existing in someone or something that's permanent and inseparable.*

The definition of *value* is *"to consider with respect to worth, merit, excellence, usefulness, or importance."*

*Inherent Value* then can be defined as worth, merit, excellence, usefulness and importance *existing within you* as permanent and inseparable.

Recognizing your Inherent Value is your key to freedom from doubting whether you matter, are capable or have value. You do. The end. This true value has always and will always exist within you. The full maturity of this understanding is to bring it fully to the surface, stand, walk and live your life with it.

Inherent Value Affirmation: *"Right here and right now, I feel and remember my inherent value, regardless of my history or circumstances."*

# 5 Steps to Knowing Your Inherent Value

*"In a time of flabby integrity, the one that is determined to live their value, knows true personal power."* – MysticMamma.com

*Inherent Value* is born within you regardless of state, stature or situation. The more I say it, the more you read it, the more the truth of it can be felt. Admittedly, this may be somewhat difficult to accept. Similarly, if you put your face up against a mirror it's hard to see your image. You have to pull back a bit to see what's right there in front of you. You're so close to this ethereal *value* that's inside you, it may be difficult to recognize. Giving it a name will help you see it, feel it and know it.

Naming your worldly *values* is a bridge to knowing your *Inherent Value. Values* can be defined as the *names* you give your principles, standards of behavior and your own judgment of what is important in life. Listed below are names of several human values.

## Naming Value:

| | |
|---|---|
| Enoughness | Creativity |
| Joy | Perseverance |
| Love | Truth |
| Fairness/Justice | Freedom |
| Respect | Responsibility |
| Harmony | Honor |
| Loyalty | Sharing |
| Honesty | Compassion |
| Integrity | Fulfillment |

1.   *Write down* your top five values from above.

2.   *Define* your chosen values in a sentence or two.

3.   *Print and post* your values as reminders in one or all of your 5 Personal Ecosystems (detailed next section).

4.   *Share* your values in a focused conversation with a close friend or family member.

5.   *Review* your values often, especially during times of doubt, fear and disempowerment.

Steps 1-5 you'll do once and review often. Daily, repeat your Inherent Value Affirmation: *"Right here and right now, I feel and remember my inherent value, regardless of my history or circumstances."* I also recommend saying this to yourself while looking in the mirror. (I prefer to say it silently to myself). Try saying it to silently to yourself and saying it out loud to see which works best for you. *Living from values leads to a valuable life.*

Knowing your *Inherent Value* and living your *chosen values* allows you to be self-possessed, self-expressed and self-determined every step of the way. It yields clarity and direction where before there was confusion and generality. Look to yourself, not the outside world for your value and validation. *The value you practice is the value you become.*

# 15

## PRACTICES FOR FOSTERING A FEELING

*"If you want to find the secrets of the universe, think in terms of energy, frequency and vibration." – Nikola Tesla*

The 2am epiphany gave me the feeling and the frequency of what became the experience of Enoughness. It was like nothing I'd felt before. It spontaneously taught me to cultivate or *foster the feeling first* for a life of true fulfillment.

The Practice of Fostering a Feeling encourages you to live a connected, creative and conscious life. Enoughness is a chosen feeling that becomes your personal barometer for relating to situations and judging their relative importance. It allows you a conscious perspective to not only creatively take life in but also give it out. By Fostering a Feeling, you become a builder of worlds from the inside out.

Jason A. Weisgerber

To help foster the chosen feeling of Enoughness are Two Practices: *Finding The Enoughnes Equilibrium* and *Creating Your Own Personal Ecosystem.*

## I. The Practice of FINDING THE ENOUGHNESS EQUILIBRIUM

Your Enoughness has always been there within you. In your heart and bones, you're very familiar with this core feeling. Now, in order to bring it to the surface, give that feeling your full attention.

## 5 Steps to the Enoughness Equilibrium

*"In every block of marble I see a statue as plain as though it stood before me, shaped and perfect in attitude and action. I have only to hew away the rough walls that imprison the lovely apparition to reveal it to the other eyes, as mine see it."* –Michelangelo

In this practice, take creative inspiration from the great Michelangelo. Your Enoughness Equilibrium and your peak life experience are the 'sculpture' that *already exists within you.* Only you know the true shape and feel, the "attitude and action" of this deep fulfillment equilibrium that's *always been*

90

*calling you.* With a practice, you can "hew away the rough walls that imprison the lovely apparition."

Remember, fulfillment is a feeling. Finding your Enoughness Equilibrium can help you shape a chosen feeling into a chosen reality. Finding the feel of it first, paying specific attention to what fulfillment feels like to you, is the first and most valuable step to living it.

(There will be natural goals you'll want to set in the Right Action & Achievement section later. Set them *from* this state of being).

*1.    Enjoy 60-Seconds of Stillness.*

Start by getting still, just as you did in steps 1-5 in the Stillness Practice above. Release your troubles. Let the world around you slowly dissolve. Come into the ease and quiet of stillness. Do this for 60-seconds.

*2.    Remember your Inherent Value.*

Enoughness is the already-ness, the innate wholeness and value with which you're born. Say to yourself again your Inherent Value Affirmation: *"Right here and right now, I feel and remember my inherent value, regardless of my history or circumstances."*

*3.   Feeling your Enoughness Equilibrium.*

This is the part where you finally take time to fully feel what's always been calling you – this deep fulfillment that frees your mind, body, spirit and voice.

Remember a moment when you felt truly fulfilled, complete and at ease. And I mean that moment when all seemed right and well in you and in the world. It could be as simple as a sunset or dynamic as a victory in court! It may be an actual memory, a picture or one imagined. It can be yours or witnessing someone else's experience that triggers the feeling in you. *Either way, have an example to refer to.*

This is simply and distinctly putting your finger on the pulse of this prime equilibrium that already and always exists right within you. No matter who you are or where you've been, you've touched and felt it before. *You can feel me talking about it right now.*

It may seem mystical and far off. It may seem, like it did for me, like you're feeling it from deep inside a cave for now. Yet it's there. Always calling you. You know this place, this sweet spot, this equilibrium. Pay full attention to it now.

For extra encouragement, remember how Maslow poetically describes the Peak Experience as *feelings of ecstasy, harmony,* and deep meaning; at one with the universe, stronger and calmer than ever before, filled with light, beauty and good. It could've been this morning, last month or years ago. You too have had glimpses and shimmerings of this peak feeling. Once you've chosen it, gently let go of the actual memory/trigger but *keep the feeling*. This is the process of remembering your own natural inner (if yet inactive) equilibrium of peace and power.

*Now name this your Enoughness.* Imagine how difficult it would be to communicate with a good friend whose name you didn't take the time to discover and remember. Feel the name - feel the connection.

4.   *Look from the End Insight.*

This is a very cool and creative step! You've just found it, named it and recaptured it. You're now the one who most intimately knows what Enoughness feels like for you. Now STEP OUT of your 'current self' for a moment and fully step into your 'Enoughness self'. Look back at your current self. *Pay attention to the personal adjustments you can make within and around your life to now match up with your Enoughness Equilibrium.* This is naturally sculpting your life the Michelangelo way. (You'll use this vision more specifically when doing your Bucket Balance Practice in the next section,

Right Action & Achievement). Use this new 'perspective' anytime to bring yourself into the shape of your Enoughness.

*Sit and absorb this feeling of your Enoughness for 10 minutes or as long as you'd like.* Now's the time to spend on finding your own feeling of optimal fulfillment. Soak it in. Let it fill every crack and crevice...

You can now let go of the practice. Relax again, breathe deep, stretch into your body and gently open your eyes.

5.    *Write It Down.*

Now write down any insights, ideas and actions related to your Enoughness Equilibrium (especially those that pop up in step 4). Take time to write freely about your experience. As you move through your life, revisit this practice often. You can also use your daily Stillness Practice to help you continually remember this feeling, this equilibrium, this experience. And in fact, recalling it any chance you get only continues to stoke the fire of your Enoughness experience.

> *"When we consider the Buddhist fly-fisherman, we intuitively know that he or she is a person who knows how **to generate who they are from the inside out**. They are, as we say, living from center. They are not in reaction to the externals of their experience –*

*the weather, the force of the current, the temperature of the water, or the amount of time they've stood standing there waiting for a nibble. They are true to their intention to catch a fish. They stand unflinching and unwavering in their commitment to align themselves with that aim."* (Emphasis added) Katherine Woodward-Thomas

# 11. The Practice of CREATING YOUR OWN PERSONAL ECOSYSTEM

*"The more we define ourselves by circumstances not to our liking, the more we delay the break-throughs and potentials that are waiting."* -Pam Younghans, Astrologer

# 5 Areas for Creating Your Own Personal Ecosystem

An ecosystem is an atmosphere or a habitat where all things are working together for the collective good. You have a *personal ecosystem* that makes up the most intimate spaces and places in your life. When you conciously take care of those areas, you're maximizing all things working together for your good for a deeply fulfilling and fully expressed life.

Take a minute and look at your office, car, home, entertainment and peer group. Do they reflect a spacious atmosphere that is supportive, creative and inspiring to living from your Enoughness? Are they inspiring your fulfillment and creativity? If not, slight adjustments can do wonders.

If you'd like, rate yourself from 1-10 in each area with 1 being least supportive and 10 being highly supportive of a fulfilling life. Then seek to bring the numbers in each area to an 8 or higher (or your chosen level) through this practice.

## 1.   *Office Space*

Is your desk clean, clear, and organized in a way that allows for great productivity, flow, and efficiency? Are the walls freshly and cleanly painted? Are there pictures on the wall to inspire and support you? Do you enjoy being there? Align the look, feel, and essence of your office (home or off-site) with the look, feel, and atmosphere of your Enoughness Equilibrium.

## 2.   *Car/Transportation*

Is your car and/or mode of transportation clean inside and out? Is the trunk of the car clear and/or organized? Is the maintenance being done in a timely manner? Are you taking preventative measures to keep your car in shape so you don't have to be surprised or unprepared for any sudden problems? Find balance in the upkeep of your car and/or mode of transportation inside and out to create another intimate space that supports the activation of your Enoughness Equilibrium.

## 3. Home/Bedroom

Is your home and bedroom clean and clear with decorations, light and colors that uplift and support you? Do you feel comfortable and able to relax? This is one of the most intimate spaces of your life. Be sure to take good care of it so it can take good care of you. Align the energy in your home/bedroom with your Enoughness Equilibrium.

## 4. Music & Entertainment

This is one of my favorite areas to adjust. It includes the music you listen to, the art you choose to see, the TV shows/films you watch, etc. Reduce energy draining music and entertainment and replace it with those that uplift and support your Enoughness Equilibrium.

## 5. Peer Group

Reduce negative conversations and people from your life. Add those that are inspiring and supportive to boost your creative potentials. This is very important yet can be difficult to navigate. Just remember the purpose behind creating a positive peer group is to help materialize your own vision for fulfillment, creative expression and your Enoughness

Equilibrium. *An intentional and supportive peer group becomes about priorities, not preferences.*

Add to the five areas if you like and find your own way. Remember that it takes a relaxed yet poised and powerful energy to find fulfillment, activate creative potential and to live well. Creating Your Own Personal Ecosystem *is vital to forwarding your cause.*

Note: Go through each of the six Life-Energy Buckets (in the following section) and take a peek at how your Personal Ecosystems are hurting or helping each bucket. *Focus on promoting energy generators while reducing and removing energy drainers.* It's smart to be in conscious command of your energy, especially in your most intimate surroundings, so your Enoughness experience is enjoyable and sustainable!

# 16

## THE PRACTICE FOR RIGHT ACTION & ACHIEVEMENT

*"Destiny is not a matter of chance but a matter of choice. It is not a thing to be waited for but a thing achieved."* – William Jennings

Right Action and Achievement points to *proof of fulfillment* as financial gains, career growth, high-functioning relationships, reaching set goals, being recognized for your gifts, talents and abilities, and other measureable results. The outer experience of Enoughness is all you would expect it to be. The enjoyment of material/outward fulfillment is a co-creative result of your ability to create feelings of fulfillment inwardly as well. A life of fulfillment and creative expression wouldn't be complete without material performance, measure and achievement.

The point is to come to accomplishments *from a healthy self-regard and a chosen experience* rather than seeking to find it in external circumstances or people. Of course, people and circumstances are vital to a healthy happy life! Yet if your fulfillment is heavily *dependent* on outer circumstances or people (which is very common), it becomes temporary and illusive. Without knowing the *inner definition and feel* of your own fulfillment, your outer fulfillment is simply a form of immediate gratification. Without the chosen inner life, outer goals are only disempowering experiences in *getting* a feeling rather than the empowered experience of *creating* one.

Right Action and Achievement, in this practice, gets its reward from being able to achieve results *beyond your circumstances or history.* Achieving goals and taking action *from Enoughness* endows you with more energy, effortlessness, grace, and impact. Right Action and Achievement comes from a well-advised, grounded beginning. It's about measureable, lasting and fulfilling results. It means *fostering a feeling* and then *acting on outcome-based goals.* This practice is where Finding Peace and Fostering a Feeling come together in a cohesive experience.

In this section you'll simply find one great practice for Right Action & Achievement: *Bucket Balance.*

# I. The Practice of BUCKET BALANCE

*"Balance and harmony aren't romantic notions but millennia old fundamentals."* – Viral Youtube Video *Enoughness: Restoring Balance to the Economy* by FirstPeoples.org

This practice helps you engage Enoughness in six distinct life-energy areas. Though this practice gets detailed and specific, always remember to pull up, live in the broad view of life and the *feel* of your Enoughness Equilibrium.

If you'd like, rate yourself from 1-10 in each bucket with 1 being least fulfilled and 10 being most fulfilled. Then seek to bring the numbers in each bucket to level 8 or higher (or your chosen level) through this practice. Here again are the six buckets.

# The 6 Life-Energy Buckets:

Imagine each bucket needs to be filled and balanced with your attention, energy and action.

## 1. Life's Work

Developing fulfillment in your work life. This includes many or all of the following qualities: *purposeful, engaging and soul-fulfilling work; financially rewarding, strongly engages your gifts and talents and provides appropriate recognition; provides room for growth and learning, inspiring challenges, creativity, vision and meaning; aligns with values, allows time to develop and implement new ideas, and has a clear social benefit. (This area can also include the awesome life's work of raising children full time).*

## 2. Self-Care, Personal Growth & Spiritual Development

*Self-Care* includes *scheduled downtime and getaways, kind and supportive self-talk, a nurturing and encouraging Personal Ecosystem (described later in Fostering a Feeling); reading and writing for fun, healthy and engaging lifestyle habits in organic nutrition and stress and energy management practices like exercise, meditation, stillness and yoga practices.*

*Personal Growth* includes *attending workshops or educational events, reading and writing for growth, having a creative outlet; volunteering, traveling and exploring higher education.*

# Enoughness

*Spiritual Development* includes *inspiring and consistent spiritual and devotional practice in prayer, meditation/stillness practice, fellowship and tithing.*

## 3. Financial Wellness

Developing fulfillment in your financial life. This includes many or all of the following qualities: *on-time bill payments, management of assets and money flow, creating strategy-driven savings and investment plans; insurance, estate planning, and long-term care; goals in increasing salary and income streams, contributing to charities and spiritual tithing.*

## 4. Intimate Relationship (includes children)

Developing fulfillment in your current or wanted intimate relationship (includes children). This includes many or all of the following qualities: *intimacy, quality, enjoyment and inspiration; shared communication, agreements, independence and definitions.*

## 5. Immediate Family

Developing fulfillment in your relationship to your immediate family. This includes many or all of the following qualities: *consistent communication, quality, enjoyment, contribution and setting appropriate boundaries with your parents,*

103

stepparents, grandparents, siblings, extended family and in-laws.

*6. Social Life*

Developing fulfillment in your social life. This includes many or all of the following qualities: *having fun for no reason, conscious and healthy friendships, shared recreation, events and celebration! This area also includes a social benefit to the planet and others, such as volunteering, recycling/reusing, and consistency in contributing to social good.*

As with the inner and outer practices of Enoughness, notice a natural overlap and synergy within these six buckets to insure your Enoughness. Feeding one bucket also feeds the others while neglecting one can deplete the others.

(*Note:* I'm an eternal advocate of getting expert guidance, coaching, and/or consulting in any area of your life where you're looking to heal, grow and evolve. There's nothing like an outside view for finding great guidance, support and direction).

## 5 Steps to Bucket Balance

In each of the six buckets, the point is to know where you are, where you're going, and how you want to feel along the way.

Take a real chunk out of a day (3+ hours) to sit down and distinctly write out your *state of affairs* in each bucket. Do this with a friend for support and inspiration if you like.

*Trust your first thought, reducing the habit of second-guessing yourself.* Move through it with momentum while not over-thinking it. Go through these steps one bucket at a time. Trust and enjoy the process. It is, after all, shaping your very destiny!

1.    *Current Actions:* List 3 things that you're *already* doing to bring fulfillment in this area of your life. It's inspiring and nourishing to your sense of motivation to recognize your current efforts.

2.    *Shorter-Term Goals:* List 3 things that you'd like to add over the next 1-6 months in this area of your life. (Example: In your Self-Care/Personal Growth/Spiritual Development Bucket, you may want to start doing yoga. This is something you can start doing within 1-6 months and doesn't take much preparation or planning). Now list 2 immediate actions under each item and the timeline you're going to take to accomplish them. And do them.

3.    *Longer-Term Goals:* List 3 things that you would like to add over the next 1-3 years in this area of your life. (Example:

In your Self-Care/Personal Growth/Spiritual Development Bucket, you may want to become a black-belt martial artist. This takes more long-term commitment, planning, and preparation). List <u>2 immediate actions</u> and the timeline you're going to take to accomplish them. And do them.

*Make sure the goals are as specific as possible and include a timeline.* "Specific" means you can *measure* them and you can *feel* them inspire you. If it feels like you're doing it by rote or without feeling, stop. Get in touch with your Enoughness Equilibrium and start again.

4. *Celebration:* When your goals are reached, celebrate! Choose the reward as a movie or dinner night out, a planned vacation, or a hot air balloon ride. Do something that allows you to let go, smile easy, blow off some steam, enjoy yourself, and *feel the satisfaction of achievement.* (Celebrate current actions as well as short and long-term achievements!).

5. *Intend to Succeed:* Now that you've clarified goals, write an *intentional success statement* to write in all buckets. It seems obvious you want to succeed. Make it overwhelmingly obvious by *writing it out.* This could be as simple as writing *"Every day I choose to feel Enoughness and enjoy success in all areas of my life."*

## WRITE IT DOWN & LET GO.

Having this practice written down helps your life balance become tangible and measurable. I suggest writing it in a personal journal or keeping a copy on your computer. And when you've done all you can in a chosen bucket, move over to another bucket. It's important to learn how to do all you can and then let go to find your balance. Sometimes big things happen when you just get out of the way!

# 17

## THE ELEPHANT IN THE ROOM
## FINANCIAL ENOUGHNESS

*"Whether you have a seven-figure trust fund or a pile of unpaid bills on your kitchen table, the path to (financial) freedom requires that you focus more on your inner life than on your outer financial circumstances."* – Brent Kessel, *It's Not About the Money*

There's a great scene in the movie *Wallstreet Never Sleeps* that applies here. The young up-and-coming stockbroker Jacob (played by Shia LaBeouf) is talking with the seasoned stockbroker Bretton (played by Josh Brolin).

*Jacob: What's your number?*

*Bretton: Excuse me?*

*Jacob: The amount of money you would need to be able to walk away from it all and just live happily-*

*ever-after. See, I find that everyone has a number and it's usually an exact number, so what's yours?*

**Bretton:** *...(Smugly) More.*

This shows one of the ways people think about money...or don't. Without considering how much is enough, you simply want *more.* This can quickly become a limitless black hole of a negative motivation that can never be filled. Yet it will eat away at you forever if you let it.

A more telling question might have been 'what' not 'how much'. *What* does fulfillment feel like or mean to you? The amount of income earned or assets owned isn't the issue in terms of living from Enoughness. It's instead about *recognizing fulfillment and knowing what you're working from, for and towards.*

Each person has a different and unique sense of finding and feeling Enoughness. You can live in Enoughness with millions of dollars in the bank, or with much less. What's important is *recognizing and experiencing fulfillment* along the way. How that creates results can be different for everyone.

Anyone interested in financial success may have, as I did, try to force it and make it happen. In forcing or 'making it happen', you might continue feeling subtly not enough, inadequate, unworthy, incomplete or un-whole *even with the accomplishments.* You haven't addressed the real issue: *What does true fulfillment feel like for you? What does it look like for you? And how will you take wise action on it?* If you don't take time to get to know what fulfillment feels like, no amount of money will ever be enough.

# INTERLUDE
# PRELIMINARY LESSONS IN
# ENOUGHNESS

## The Bangkok Mafia

Enoughness is a compass that can help give you a healthy focus, meaning and direction. It's your compass, your natural sense of true fulfillment and creative expression that brings you to Enoughness. Before I had that compass restored, I did some foolish things that helped begin to uncover my own misdirection and reveal a newfound sense of true fulfillment, meaning and direction. By accident. Foolish. Key words here.

One of these lessons came when I was doing a month long trek through Thailand and, along the way, *accidentally* got involved with the Bangkok Mafia. It was a bit like a *Mission*

*Impossible* movie: a very intense and unnerving adventure. Admittedly, an adventure for fools. I think maybe innocence lost can also lead to foolishness. Innocence restored, as in the case of my Enoughness awakening, becomes wisdom.

I had just graduated from the 2-year NYC acting conservatory. I was exhausted and decided to get away, rest and rejuvenate. It was the first time I'd traveled outside the United States, other than a quick trip to Mexico in College where I *innocently/foolishly* got arrested and spent a frightening night in jail. That's another story.

## Arriving in Bangkok

I arrived in Bangkok late at night. I had been given useful advice from other friends on traveling through Thailand. They gave me suggestions on where to visit and how to negotiate prices for rooms, clothing, food, tours, taxis, and tuk-tuks (Thailand's open-air three-wheeled city taxis).

Though I was glad to get insights from other travelers, I made a promise to myself to stay open to new experiences. I wanted to dive deep into the Thai culture and learn more about myself along the way. And I wanted to do it safely. I set simple boundaries: no drugs, prostitution or other unhealthy exploits!

After landing, I grabbed a taxi, negotiated a reasonable price, and went straight to my pre-arranged rented bungalow. Since it was late and I was exhausted from traveling for more than eighteen hours, I said thank you to my hosts and went up to my room.

It was a small 10' x 10' room with a single bunk and a small nightstand. It was all the room I needed. I was only planning on staying a couple nights before heading out to the islands. I went straight to sleep.

*First Day*

My first day, I woke up early, equally excited and apprehensive about what might lie ahead. My plan was to explore Bangkok for a day or two, then disappear for a few weeks into the islands and mountains. Other than a general plan, I'd let my trip unfold naturally.

I was within walking distance of a highly frequented tourist area with a market and a small Buddhist temple. I decided to start there. As soon as I stepped out on the street I was overwhelmed and confused. The traffic seemed to go in all directions and there were people everywhere. Although at six feet, I was taller than almost anyone around me, I couldn't see where to cross the street! As I paused trying to take it all in, a Thai man dressed in a suit suddenly appeared next to me.

I noticed right away he spoke fluent English. He said hello and asked if I was visiting from the United States. I obviously stood out. I was glad to connect and told him I was just in from New York to explore Thailand for a few weeks. He welcomed me and confirmed the streets were confusing, offering to walk part way with me.

As we walked and made small talk, he mentioned this day was the last day of a special Buddhist holiday. Apparently, the city was offering discounted tours to many of the sacred temples and other city monuments. Without any particular plans, I agreed to take the tour. The cost was about 300 Thai Baht, which was then about $10 US dollars for a half-day trip in one of the three-wheeled tuk-tuks. I liked the sound of it, and it fit well into my minimalistic travelers' budget. Not only that, I sometimes had a hard time saying no. Possibly the result of a depleted core, feelings of inadequacy and not-enoughness.

He described most of the stops on the tour and it all seemed like a great way to be introduced to Bangkok. He mentioned that at the end of the tour, the tuk-tuk would take me to a jewelry store for discounted deals on jewelry. Though it sounded strange, I didn't think much of it. He assured me that although it was a required stop on the trip, I didn't have to buy anything. He made it easy for me as he quickly whistled to a passing tuk-tuk and immediately got me a ride. I was off and riding.

*Tuk-Tuk Tour – Romancing the Tourist*

Indeed I did stop at some great sites along the way. I saw the historical Golden Buddha, the world's largest solid gold statue, in the Wat Traimit temple. It was a beautiful, peace-filled experience. I also stopped at another temple with a 50-foot Buddha sculpture lying on its side, Buddha's last posture before taking his death and entering Nirvana. It was a sweetly humbling site.

Even in all the hustle, I noticed there was a sacred feel to the city. In the U.S. we have ATMs on every corner. Bangkok seemed instead to have small temples or open-air prayer sites on every corner. It was as though people were praying, lighting incense, and making spiritual offerings at all times of the day. I was soaking it all in (including the delicious *exhaust* from the jam-packed traffic) as we ripped across town in this three-wheeled madness.

At one point, we stopped at another temple. I was taking off my shoes to enter when two men taking photos of the area paused to talk to me. They were American, from San Francisco. We talked for a bit about our travels and what was ahead.

They were both frequent travelers. One of them asked if I was on the tuk-tuk holiday tour; I said yes and explained that I had already seen a few of the other grand sites around town. One of them told me he too had done this tour the first time he came to Thailand. He told me he really enjoyed the tour. And he made it clear he hadn't planned on buying any jewelry as it sounded like a scam.

I was surprised to learn he actually decided to buy jewelry on the tour after all. He reasoned that by sending it immediately to his sister in San Francisco to sell for him, he'd hoped it would help pay for his trip. And apparently his sister was able to sell it at a good price and it actually paid for his entire trip. He added that while in Bangkok, he still buys jewelry priced low and sells high, just to fund his trip.

While I was still not focused on jewelry, it added to the intrigue as I considered his story.

*The Jewelry – Made in Mafia*

As the tour was coming to an end, I was finally taken to a small jewelry store. It was in a typical strip mall. The tuk-tuk driver dropped me off and left as I entered the store. I thought it was unusual because at every other site he'd stayed outside and waited for me. I figured he'd return to take me back to my bungalow.

As I came to the front of the building, there were two big men in suits guarding the store. This seemed normal enough to me. After all, it was a jewelry store. One of them opened the door for me and I entered into a narrow, dimly lit, and starkly decorated room with one or two women standing behind some empty glass counters.

One of the women in a smart business suit greeted me with all smiles. She welcomed me to a chair in front of one of the cases. I thought I'd just stand and get this over with quickly, but the invite to sit in the chair seemed more like an order than an offer.

She talked with me casually for a few minutes. I soon felt a strange pressure as she began to discuss my options in buying high quality jewelry at low prices. It was as if the decision had already been made for me. Looking back, I'd say it had.

I didn't know my own mind very well at that time. *And when you don't know your own mind, it becomes easy for others to know it for you.* It's much easier to take advantage of an indecisive, misdirected, and unconscious mind. It's also easier to take advantage of a deeply unhappy, discontented and disheartened person whose chronically looking for a quick fix.

Reading me well, she walked me through the higher priced diamonds quickly and then came to the more accessible blue sapphire sets. I told her quickly that I wasn't really interested and was traveling on a tight budget. Again, she was very sweet and very professional. She began telling me stories about how other travelers had come through many times buying jewelry at incredible deals and selling them for a profit in the United States. It sounded good but I was still resistant.

It was then she seemed to pull out the big negotiating guns. She aggressively pushed a set of jewelry that included blue sapphire earrings, a pendant, and a ring. She insisted this was the best deal she had. She also conveniently offered to help me sell it in New York, my current state of residence.

Out of nowhere, she quickly gave me a printed sheet listing the different jewelry stores in Manhattan. She said almost all the stores on the list had bought jewelry from her before. She gave me her business card and said *she'd personally help me sell the jewelry* if I had any trouble.

Finally, she told me I could return it to her for a small fee by mail if I couldn't find a buyer within 30 days. I was quickly losing excuses to say no. I felt guilty for hesitating! I started to sweat. Then I started to wonder.

She had me. And she knew it.

I thought I could handle it. And I wanted to trust her. I wanted to trust myself! Of course, there was part of me that also wanted to take the risk to pull it off and make some quick cash. Feelings of not-enoughness slowly began to creep in and help me make decisions.

I thought it would be a risk I was willing to take…for $3000. I put the charge on my credit card and filled out all the papers. I quickly spent money I didn't have. The desperate and insecure gambler in me thought it might be worth the stretch to make a quick buck.

The woman that sold me the jewelry highly recommended mailing it home right away in order to secure the jewelry. Smart. I watched them seal the package. I signed off on the papers and sent the jewelry home to my family in the U.S. Before I knew it, I'd made the purchase.

*Escort, Massage, and Dinner for Fools*

As a sign of "appreciation" for doing business with them, the jewelry storeowners wanted to send me out for a nice dinner. That was nice of them. They called in an escort, a woman near my age, to pick me up. For the sake of anonymity, I'll call her Mai. I wondered if this was some sort of glorified prostitution offering?

Mai picked me up in her used Honda Civic, with a couple friends in the back seat. There was American pop music on the radio, everyone was smiling and singing...it was a small party in the car! And my hosts were there to share the fun. This was no prostitution story but a real gesture to thank me for my business. It helped take my mind off the money I just spent. Smart.

Their plan was to take me out to enjoy an authentic Thai dinner and to some hip nightclubs. But first they took me to get a massage. I hesitated, thinking - what am I getting into? I had made the vow to be open to all experiences, but drugs and/or prostitution were definitely out. Again, it was a legitimate gratitude offering as a standard Thai massage.

Afterwards, we jumped back in the car and went straight to a nearby restaurant for dinner. The place was huge and had a massive outdoor eating area. We sat down at one of the outdoor tables right next to what looked like a small lake. It turned out the lake was man-made, used to hold the live shrimp and fish that the restaurant served. We were given small fishing poles with a simple hook at the end of a line and some kind of bait. I was feeling more and more at ease. Mai was respectfully friendly with me and I felt genuinely welcomed.

(All of this was a trust challenge – for trust in myself and subsequently of others through these complete strangers from across the globe. It all tested my intuitive ability to know the genuine from ingenuine, in me and around me. I'd say my intuitive life was mainly dormant and depressed until this Bangkok experience peaked my interest, curiousity and caution. I'd say I needed the wake up call, at any cost. If I look back at it as healing to my intuitive body, this whole experience probably saved me countless hours in talk therapy! Not to mention money).

The restaurant they took me to was unusually enchanting. We ordered some food and caught some small fish to be cooked by the chefs in the restaurant. I think I was the only white person in the place. Again, it felt like the curtain had been drawn and I was experiencing an *authentic* night out with the locals at one of their hot spots.

This was the dive into the local Thai culture I was seeking. Mai, her friends and I were all having a great time. It continued late into the night as I thoroughly enjoyed the very uncommon (to me) music and conversation. I was finally exhausted and ready to go home.

Mai drove and dropped her friends off first. On the way back to my bungalow, Mai told me about her son. She said she was very close with him, that in fact, he's changed her life. It had grounded her and given her focus, purpose and strength. She went on to tell me that everything she does is for him and she's never been happier. A genuine and relatable love.

I thanked her for treating me so kindly and for taking me out. Though she said it was unusual, she invited me to contact her if I were ever back in Bangkok. She gave me a business card with her name and cell phone number on it, and said goodnight.

At this point, my trip had started strong and I was feeling good. I'd soon realize I hadn't fully dealt with my demons. And because of that, I made a big mistake. I had a deep emptiness in me and didn't know how to deal with it. I was truly lost. And worst of all, I was looking for a quick fix that I knew didn't really exist.

## Beware! Bangkok Mafia – Pay Attention to the Signs

It was a full first day. After Mai dropped me off, I walked straight up to my bungalow to go to sleep. I turned on the lights and put my pack down. As I closed the door, I noticed on the back of it a laminated sign with a lengthy memo. As I read it, I felt the blood rush out of my body and my heart sink in panic.

*"Beware of jewelry scams! ...Bangkok Mafia..."* It went on to almost exactly describe the experience I just had. (It also described similar scams with travel agencies that didn't exist, selling train tickets and flights to nearby tourist destinations).

I was sunk. My first day out and I had just let myself be scammed out of $3000 I didn't have to buy fake jewelry. Even as I write about it now, it seems nuts to fall for it. Looking back, it was a finely orchestrated process.

At least I'd like to believe it was finely orchestrated; the man on the corner...the convenient Buddhist holiday tour...the two American travelers at the temple...the slick saleswoman and her promise to help. And then a gracious night out with some friendly locals to seal the deal.

The intricacy of the scam actually impresses me now. Back then it felt like global betrayal! They seemed to really know how to play on the perfect storm of my insecurity, greed and ignorance.

Underneath it all, I was feeling hurt, humiliated, ashamed, and embarrassed. I'd felt this sting of worldly betrayal before with the knife attack at 11 years old. When I was younger, I didn't ask for it. In a way, this time, I had. Maybe I was subconsciously seeking a chance to find justice as an adult that I didn't have as a kid.

## The Sapphire Truth – Finding Justice

Once blood returned to my brain, I remembered Mai had given me her business card. It was late, but I went straight back down to the reception area to use the house phone. Since it was a house phone, I had to get permission to use it.

There was still one of the staff members awake, patrolling the grounds. I got his attention and told him my story. When I did, he shook his head with a stern look of great disappointment on his face. *"Why did you do this?! Didn't you read the warning in your room? We do our best to protect travelers from this kind of activity but you must pay attention!"*

I was surprised at his direct lecture but I could see he actually cared for my safety and well-being as his guest. He asked why I wanted to use the phone, what good would it do this late night? I told him I had the phone number of one of the people involved and would like to try to get her help. He thought it was crazy, but he helped me anyway.

Surprisingly, Mai answered the phone. I said a quick hello and went straight to the point. Was it true? Was it all a scam? After a bit of silence she said *"I'm sorry, Jason. I really like you, you're a very nice guy...but yes, this is as you say."*

*"So the jewelry is fake and this is all a scam??"* I shouted. Again, she confirmed it. For some reason, I was shocked all over again. She admitted the jewelry was fake and it was all a scam. I had no choice but take full responsibility for my actions. While Mai wasn't taking any blame, she somehow still offered a caring ear.

I was beginning to see a pattern. Caring can show up even in the midst of betrayal. And I didn't have to feel alone, even in a foreign country. I was equally frightened and calmed.

I was confused and didn't know what to do next. I was immature, naïve, Western and lacking in cultural wisdom. I guess I thought she'd take it from there and give me good "customer service" while helping to get my money back. So Western. My expectations were fruitless and silly. Justice wouldn't be that easy.

I continued to try to talk to her, telling her the money I spent was money I didn't have and I desperately needed to get it back. I was persistent and pushed hard. She told me this was a system very closely controlled by the *Bangkok Mafia* and she couldn't help. Ouch. And yikes.

She reminded me that she has a young son, that the father of her child isn't helping her, and this is some of the only work she can get to support herself and her son. She understood desperation better than I. She said that even talking on the phone like this would put her and her son in danger. I didn't know what to believe.

In all this, Mai remained calm. She was very patient and responsive. Maybe she'd been through this before? It was already a deep learning experience for me. I heard this woman clearly stand her ground, essentially telling me *no*, yet not backing away or having me feel wrong for asking.

# Enoughness

Other than those few hours out, she and I were complete strangers from very different parts of the world. Yet she never left me feeling disconnected and alone. What a gift. Even as she said no, essentially rejecting me, she didn't disconnect. She offered a strong, grounded stance along with an unspoken compassion that I had not felt before and certainly not from a stranger. I'm sure this isn't the first time she'd had to endure guilt in order to take care of her family. I could feel her regret as well as her resignation to her limited choices.

I eased up. I thanked her for listening. I asked one more time if there was anything she could do to help me. She breathed a deep sigh of frustration and was quiet again for a few moments. I listened with great care...no longer pushing, but openly and respectfully asking.

I was ready for her to say no. In those brief moments, she taught me how to let go and still proceed towards my aim, which I now see is a very fine art. Her lifestyle likely required the mastery of this skill. In her case, it was the difference between money and danger.

Mai asked me how long I was going to be in Bangkok. I told her I was on my way to the islands the next day but was scheduled to be back in Bangkok in a few weeks to fly home. I offered to stay in Bangkok. With hesitation, she told me to go on my trip. It would give this thing time to cool down. She asked me to contact her again when back in Bangkok and she'd do her best to help get my money back.

Mai also told me to have the jewelry sent back to me, which might help in negotiating the exchange. I immediately emailed my family to have it sent back to the bungalows. It arrived and was waiting for me at the bungalows by the time I returned to Bangkok. Before I hung up, she reminded me again that she was putting herself, and possibly me, in danger. She didn't have to remind me to be careful.

I whole-heartedly agreed with everything she suggested. Though I hesitated on whether I should pursue this with both her safety and mine in danger, I was ready to move forward. At this point, I was on a mission to get my money back and to unwittingly find justice.

The next day, I traveled by ferry over to the island of Koh Samui with the shame of the recent sting still lingering. Though my trip started off on a low note, my time on the islands and in the mountains was magical. Perhaps the fear of returning to Bangkok fueled my enjoyment and peaked my attention. I felt the strange mix of fear and elation driving me onward.

I stayed on the island for a couple weeks before traveling up to spend a week in the mountains of Pai. Though my time on the islands and moutains of Thailand was very sweet, I was feeling the itch to get back to Bangkok. It was time to go.

# Back in Bangkok

When I got back into Bangkok, I stayed at the same bungalows. I got settled in and called Mai. She answered, we greeted, and it was down to business. The jewelry had arrived and I was ready to go.

Mai started by giving me the name of the shopping center where I originally bought the jewelry. She asked me to go back to the store right away and ask for my money back. She told me to be very careful and respectful but to also hold my ground and be strong. She advised that I let them know I'm not satisfied with the transaction and that I'd like a full refund. I was not to accuse them of anything, just go through the steps of asking for a return.

*First Mission – Revisit the Storefront*

I did what Mai asked me to do. That very day, I had a tuk-tuk take me back to the shopping center. When I got there, the jewelry shop had vanished. The retail space was completely empty and there were vacancy signs on the windows.

I thought I had the wrong place so I went back to the bungalows and called Mai to let her know. She wasn't surprised. She told me that it's common for them to switch locations frequently. Mai asked me to call her back the next day so she could try to find out where they'd moved.

*Second Mission – New Store, Same Story*

Early the next day I called again. Mai found the new location. Again, she had to remind me to be careful. She asked me never to mention her name or how I got this information. Again I agreed. I wondered if I was just getting this kind woman and myself into more trouble? Or maybe she was setting me up. But I was in this now, and I was hell-bent on following through.

She gave me the address to the new location. I jumped in a tuk-tuk again and went straight there. As I walked up, I noticed the same two oversized guards at the front doors. I went to walk in and they quickly stopped me.

The guards asked if they could help me. I said I was there to return my jewelry. I had my backpack on with the fake jewelry inside and was ready to turn it over. They said the store was invite only and they couldn't help me.

I was already frustrated and fed up, so I bravely said *"I recognize both of you from the last store. I know this is a scam. I just want my money back."* I thought maybe I pushed it too much. Naivety was driving me, which probably played in my favor!

They asked me to sit down on a nearby bench and wait outside for a moment while one of them went inside. I sat there sweating for 30 minutes, both from the hot sticky weather and the fear of what might happen next. The guard came back out, opened the door and told me to go up the stairs in the back.

Here I am a young, naive American trekking in Thailand alone with my backpack. No one knows where I am and I'm going to the back stairs of the Bangkok Mafia's fake jewelry store. It could only get better from here. Or worse.

I climbed the stairs and came to an open door. An older, well-dressed and fairly distinguished gentleman sat inside behind a desk at the far end of the room. He gestured me inside with an easy smile. In any usual situation, that smile would've eased my nerves. His smile was subtly meant to make me *unnerved.* And it did. But I was determined to figure this out.

I went inside. The room was long and narrow with damp lighting. There was nothing else in the room but the big desk this man was sitting behind and a metal chair in front of it. I walked over, took my backpack off, and sat down as he kindly asked me what he could do for me.

Very respectfully, I let him know that I'd bought some jewelry by mistake, had paid with money I didn't have, and that I needed to return it. I told him that I heard a rumor that the jewelry may be of no actual value and I just wanted to return it. I was trying to hint at the truth while playing it safe. He asked me if I had the jewelry with me.

This made me nervous again, thinking *"what if they just take the jewelry now and I'll have nothing to show for it? What if they just take it, beat me up, and dump me somewhere?"* I relented and said yes. He asked how much I paid and I showed him the receipt.

Kindly, he shared that since I'd already mailed it across borders, he had no way of proving that this was the actual jewelry sold by his company. Even though the seal had clearly not been broken, the only thing he could do for me was to give me $100.00 in cash and take the jewelry back.

What a clever response. He wasn't taking me seriously. He just wanted me gone.

I didn't accept. He quickly thanked me, wished me well, and suggested I go. Mai had coached me on not pushing too hard. This one was easy. I pushed once. With this guy, in this situation, once was clearly (and safely) enough. I went home and hoped Mai had another idea.

*Third Mission – Police Report*

The time spent on this was adding up. I had to postpone my flight back to the U.S. to continue the mission. The next day brought good news as I told Mai what happened. She helped me get my confidence back when she told me she'd heard a report from her 'employers' that someone was trying to return jewelry. Apparently they didn't like me snooping around. She said this would be good leverage because, in the end, they wanted to avoid attention.

She guided me to the next step, which was to go to the police station and report it. Mai said it wouldn't do much good. There was corruption everywhere. However, she knew I'd need an official police report, even one that made no difference, in order to go the next step.

I did what she told me to do and filed a police report. When I was done, I called to share the day's accomplishments with Mai. By now, she and I were partners with a plan. I had hope for redemption. Now it was time for the next and final step: going to an international governmental liaison to file a report and make the final effort.

*Fourth Mission – Humble Victory*

With Mai's specific instructions, the next day I went to a government-type office building. I didn't pay attention to details at this point. I wanted to get this done. *"Bring the jewelry. Show them the copy of your police report. File another report there and be very strong about it but be very careful. They know you're following up on this."*

This time I was in an office that felt much more diplomatic than the police station. The gentleman who helped me asked if I'd filed a police report and I showed him the copy. I also told him that I'd tried returning the jewelry personally without success. He had me sit outside his office and fill out another report.

When I finished, he looked over all of my information. He let me know that, unfortunately, this kind of thing happens often and there wasn't much he could do. He also hinted that they do their best to warn travelers about these scams. He was trying to make me feel ashamed for my mistake. I didn't need help with that part. This wasn't going as I expected and I was growing weary.

Finally, he shook his head and told me there was nothing he could do. I was ready to give up. He asked if I would wait outside while he finished up the report.

While I was outside, I called Mai on a payphone to let fill her in. She got frantic and told me to go back into his office and demand to get half my money back *in cash. "Tell him you won't leave the country until you get your money back!"* She said the people she worked for were fed up with my pursuits and wanted it to stop. She said they gave him half the money in cash ($1500.00) to send me away - he's saying no so he can keep the money for himself!

Frustrated and tired, I reluctantly went back. When I was asked to come into the office, I sat down and before he could say anything, I told him exactly what Mai advised me to tell him - I wouldn't leave the country until I got half my money back in cash. I added that I was keeping the jewelry. At this point, it didn't make a difference.

I took a chance and even alluded to the fact that I knew he had the money, because I didn't quite believe it! He asked me to give him another few minutes and wait outside while he took another look at my reports.

Sure enough, as he invited me back in, he looked at me for a few ticks and opened his desk drawer. He pulled out a simple white envelope stuffed with cash. He slid it across his desk and advised me to be on my way. I didn't need to count it as I put the envelope full of cash in my backpack. I thanked him and assured him that I was happy to be on the next flight home.

I left the building and walked ever so cautiously and quickly. It was a very *mindful* walk. I felt elated, frightened, and grateful all at the same time. I had a slight feeling of triumph coated in heavy humility. And I was ready to go home.

I went to the nearby tourist spot that was my intended destination on that first day in Bangkok. I was back at the beginning. I sat at a restaurant, had some water, took a deep breath and let it all go.

I called Mai to thank her profusely. I asked to get her address so I could send her some money. She declined, wished me well and quickly hung up. It was done. I picked up my backpack and went back to the bungalows. I packed up the rest of my things, took a cab to the airport and flew home.

# The Story of a Lifetime

I value my Bangkok experience in so many ways. And I couldn't have better written the story by making it up! There could've been no better, no safer, no clearer, no truer experience that could've taught me so much about myself, about life, and about others. There's no better teacher than experience.

Looking back, watching that last government official blatantly lie, and then fess up, was an eye opening experience. He was technically the authority. I was meant to follow his lead. This moment empowered me to reclaim my own authority and allowed me to heal a bit more from the disempowering experiences I had growing up.

And I got the adventure, the life lesson, and the story of a lifetime as a reward. I even got an extra 50 bucks in my pocket when I finally sold the jewelry to a pawnshop in Los Angeles!

Rich man. Rich in experience. Though I didn't feel much more than neutral about it all, in the end, justice was served.

A year later I was to have a life-changing, dynamic and illuminating late night awakening in a Los Angeles city park. I believe the Bangkok redemption was the initiation. I felt a new, real fulfillment and peace as I traveled the remote islands of Koh Samui. I felt closer to God again as I traveled through the glorious mountains of Pai. And I felt a sense of capability and inner human strength awaken as I chased down my jewelry justice in Bangkok. It was perhaps the seeds of Enoughness getting their first breath of life.

# 18

## THE EVOLUTION OF EXPERIENCE

In the fullest experience of Enoughness, you can feel at peace, deeply fulfilled, intuitively creative and capable of handling whatever comes your way. You can fully enjoy and engage in your daily experience while learning something about your self and your dreams along the way. Experience is a grand test of life that can never really be failed. So lean into it, stand up for yourself and expect life to always be interesting! And have a creative practice to rely on, to remind you and to support you every step of the way.

With a solid practice, you no longer have to sleepwalk through life, feeling lost, unfulfilled, disconnected or unexpressed. You can *flip your perspective* to Enoughness at any time and let it slowly but surely sweetly color your view again. *And ultimately, you can tap into the intuitive power of fostering a feeling until it blooms fully into your reality.* What a smart way to *choose* to live. This is the evolution of experience.

*This is true fulfillment and a fully expressed life.*

With your Enoughness Equilibrium in tact, you're no longer on the sidelines of life. Instead, you're right there in the middle of it all, making your own decisions and having a unique influence on the book of life. At the core of it all, leading you, inspiring you and empowering you - is your Enoughness.

*This is true fulfillment and a fully expressed life.*

Evolving in this way means shedding off the cocoon of darkness, mis-education, inauthentic interests, overwhelm, under-whelm, and false feelings of not-enoughness. You're shedding the lost, limited, empty and separated 'outsider' or 'over compensator' experience most people know too well. *With your Enoughness in tact,* you can feel finally at home in your skin, clear and capable of creating a chosen life.

*This is true fulfillment and a fully expressed life.*

You become not "new and improved." *You become outwardly all that you already are inwardly* - scars, snot, and dirt; ignorance, intelligence, and genius; capability, competency, and quirk-icity. The ugly and the beautiful. The failures and the successes. The invincibility and the fragility. The impenetrability and the vulnerability. *You become you.* Back to the beginning and forward again. Coming full...circle.

*Know yourself again for the first time with this restored innocence.* Remember this over and over and over until it lifts you up to your level, your peak, your Enoughness.

# 19

## PROGRESS FROM FULFILLMENT

Enoughness is a state of being that's meant to move you forward in life. It's meant to feed you into the *graceful* stream of life and leave behind the *struggle*. Sound good?

The secret is out. *There IS a central and peak experience in life.* There IS a powerful and natural equilibrium for fulfillment and creativity *already living within you.* It's attainable and accessible. And it's up *you* to bring it fully forward now. I'm sure you wouldn't have it any other way!

I had a funny thought about all this - some folks think finding deep fulfillment and true satisfaction will mean the end of motivation. *That's a bit like believing that being full once means you'll never be hungry again.* Funny. You may think it means growth and progess become stagnant, leaving you behind the times. Not funny!

However, I can attest that when hunger is truly satisfied, even just once, a whole world opens up. A *whole*...world. A flourishing, honey-soaked, dynamically alive and inviting world *opens up for you in fulfillment*. Not the other way around.

And that's because now you've actually experienced true fulfillment. Now you know what you're looking for and what it feels like inside and out. Next time, you'll be able to repeat it easier than before.

There's a vibrant, inviting and fitting territory that is *ever-expanding* and calling for you to explore, enjoy and accomplish. And yes of course you'll have to eat again! Yet now you'll know what it feels like to be sweetly and uniquely quenched, quelled and calmed. And now, rather than simply repeating the search for dissatisfaction, you can further than ever before.

And here's a secret: I know that you know that experiencing this *deep quench* is what you've always wanted. It's the golden lining to living life. Time now to step *up* to it, step *into* it and *get* it. Be brave and allow, engage and *live*...in this deep fulfillment.

# Enoughness

*Enoughness isn't the end of passion; it's a foundation for it.* Many people are now living fulfilled, creatively expressed, alive and well in their lives. You can include me on that list. What about you? The experience and practice of Enoughness seeks to give that hungry heart of yours a tasty, filling dose of what it wants most so it can *open up and let the best of what's already inside you – out.* This fulfillment is the smart point of progress for your life now and always.

# 20

## THE NEW CALL

*Enoughness is the healthy alternative to the limiting experiences of settling for less or being addicted to more.* In the end, true fulfillment is possible. Get it. It's your inner peace, awakened equilibrium and creative achievements that conjure the fulfillment of your greatest life. I'm catching the fire. I'm sharing the secret. And I'm being the change I wish to see (and feel) in the world. How about you?

*Enoughness is your home*, free of any exaggerated sense of lack and inadequacy. Build it. Start by *building a home* before building a city.

There's a part of Enoughness that you already own, and a part you earn. There's a part of Enoughness that you already are and a part you become. There's a part you embrace and a part you practice.

The Practice of Finding Peace is found in your *Stillness Practice and Knowing your Inherent Value*. The Practice of Fostering a Feeling means finding your *Enoughness Equilibrium* and *Creating Your Own Personal Ecosystem*. And the Practice of Right Action and Achievement begins and ends with your life's *Bucket Balance*.

Let go of what's not moving you forward. Instead, search out and embrace all things that are supporting your call to a *life lived fully,* in and from your Enoughness. Believe it. And believe in yourself! Remember this until your dying day - and beyond.

I'm wishing you well. I'm wishing the best of life for you and life the best of you. Here's to your fullest experience of Enoughness.

**Enoughness**

# Appendix

## The Promise Remembered

There's something that needs to be remembered. It's something that's good to remember at any age, from any background and in any situation. It's the remembrance of Enoughness.

━━

*In your Enoughness, you are never alone.*

*And when you need help, it will always be there in some way.*

*Drink this into your soul and be deeply quenched.*

━━

*Whenever needed, start again, on your knees if you must.*

*Then come out of the dark heaviness and into to the sweetness of light.*

*Heal, grow and live again.*

━━

*Gently, care-fully and repeatedly*

*take up the reins and stand as the righteous heir of your life ~*

*the heir that you already are, have always been and will always be.*

⟋⟋

*Take up and wear,*

*with courage and confidence,*

*the crown of your Enoughness.*

⟋⟋

*The promise remembered is the promise fulfilled.*

*It is the life originally and always meant for you.*

*It is your ability to go beyond healing,*

*into the redemption of a natural and flourishing life.*

⟋⟋

*Believe it. Receive it. Share it.*

*Welcome to the fullness of life. Welcome to your Enoughness.*

⟋⟋

# ABOUT THE AUTHOR

JASON A. WEISGERBER is an author and keynote speaker. He is also the creator and host of the online audio series, *The Enoughness Sessions*.

Jason has an eclectic educational background as a professionally trained actor with a degree in Business as well as a Theological Masters in The Evolution of Consciousness. He is equally self-taught and formally educated.

Jason's belief is that a full life includes the right mix of personal peace, self-expression and measured accomplishment – otherwise known as Enoughness. He has combined his love of art, business, spiritual development, personal growth and education to do his part in the progress of caring human development and positive social change. He is ever a student of life and a lover of nature.

*www.EnoughnessSessions.com*

*Jason@JasonWeisgerber.com*